THE ART OF DISARMING

THE ART OF DISARMING

Steve Tarani

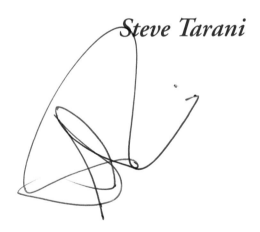

EMPIRE Books

P.O. Box 491788, Los Angeles, CA 90049

First published in 2008 by Empire Books

First edition

08 07 06 05 04 03 02 01 00 99 1 3 5 7 9 10 8 6 4 2

Printed in the United States of America.

Empire Books
P.O. Box 491788
Los Angeles, CA 90049

Library of Congress Cataloging-in-Publication Data

ISBN-13: 978-1-933901-41-1
ISBN-10: 1-933901-41-1

Library of Congress Cataloging-in-Publication Data

Tarani, Steve, 1961-
  The art of disarming / by Steve Tarani. -- 1st ed.
     p. cm.
  ISBN-13: 978-1-933901-41-1 (pbk. : alk. paper)
  ISBN-10: 1-933901-41-1
  1. Knife fighting. 2. Self-defense. I. Title.
  GV1150.7.T35 2008
  613.6'6--dc22
                              2008015792

ACKNOWLEDGEMENTS

It is with respect and honor that the author acknowledges the true masters of the blade and conservators of the ancient arts from which all of this material was derived. Listed in alphabetical order: Grandmaster Leovigildo Miguel Giron, Grandmaster Tatang Illustrisimo, Guro Dan Inosanto, Master Dexter Labanog, Guro Ted Lucaylucay, Master Christopher Ricketts, Punong Guro Edgar G. Sulite, Master Tony Somera, and Pendekar/Guru Besar Herman Suwanda.

The author also acknowledges the personal effort and tremendous contribution of Guro John Spezzano who volunteered his personal time and service as a professional editor of this material. Editing manuscripts is a mind-altering task that takes countless hours and endless read-through—and in some cases an entire re-write! Thanks again brother John for hammering through the many grueling hours.

The author additionally acknowledges Barry Shreiar, who without his generosity in bending of Einstein's time-space continuum this project would never have made it off the ground. A resounding salamat also to Paul "Ted" "Bubba" Grybow and Tim Egberts (who are both graduate instructors of the Bahala Na System—Stockton, CA) for their assistance and support throughout the project.

Last but certainly not least to Rebecca Lynn Day (aka "MGLSB") for her help and efforts in illustrations and project preparations.

CONTENTS

FOREWORD

In the past decade and a half (as of this writing) as a professional personal safety instructor throughout the professional training community it is part of my job responsibilities to relay various training components including personal defense against an attack with an edged weapon. As a direct result of numerous questions regarding the art of disarming posed by many students of all backgrounds and levels of training over the decades, this manuscript was composed to provide a cursory response.

The techniques and concepts contained herein are derived via the more than 25 years of my life devoted to the study of the bladed arts training under the masters listed above. To this very day I spend as much time as possible under their direct tutelage. The material was passed along to them by their teachers and to them by their teachers and so on back deep into history. Most of the training technology was passed down the long corridors of time by oral tradition alone.

Having trained in the US as well as Japan, the Philippines and Indonesia, it is my humble opinion that these aforementioned masters are true conservators of the ancient bladed arts. It is by their generosity and sharing of combative concepts and techniques that any of this material survives to this modern age, a debt that can never be repaid. It is the access to the teachings of these masters in a single manuscript that may benefit the reader with reference to the art of disarming.

INTRODUCTION

Imagine the dawn of man, literally scratching out an existence as a gatherer (possibly hunter) of resources (food, water, etc.) critical to his survival.

Along came the first human predator that requires and of course desired those same exact resources and decided to take them by force. Clenching his unwashed, hair covered hand, into a closed fist or perhaps with the back of his calloused hand he forcefully smashes his fellow human being in the head with enough force to send him tumbling backwards ushering in the beginning of human conflict.

As the millennia passed, man found more improved methods of damaging his fellow man. Impact weapons such as sticks and stones were the very first hand-held implements which increased effectiveness. Later on came the edged weapon—sharp spears, arrows, and eventually battle axes, swords and daggers which proved to be far more effective at destroying another human being than impact weapons. In fact edged weapons are still used to this very day.

Following the invention and subsequent usage of gunpowder to launch projectiles by the Chinese (first documented around 12th century AD) the firearm although in it's embryonic stages (the matchlock of the 1400's, the wheel-lock of the 1500's, the flintlock of the 1600's) was still not employed widely until the late 17th century and even then the sword and dagger remained dominant in the world of weapons. It wasn't really until near the beginning of the 19th century with the advent of the percussion cap (invented by the Reverend John Forsyth in around 1825) when firearms surpassed edged weapons and took the lead as a superior weapon.

Ironically throughout history, the only mechanics that have changed in the never-ending saga of human conflict is technology. Even today resources such as land, food, and fossil fuels remain an impetus to the continuation of that first brain-housing smashing those millennia ago.

Given that necessity is the mother of invention, it logically follows that weapons technology is paralleled and in some cases further developed by the need of weapons application. The opposite is never true. For example if you were hypothetically able to place an actual Neanderthal or Cro-Magnon in the weapons bay of a modern nuclear submarine and ordered him to launch a missile he would most likely grunt and (of course once trained) would eagerly complete the task. Conversely if you placed the average nuclear weapons specialist in a loincloth, handed him a spear and asked him to survive in the middle of 40,000 BC no doubt he would most likely echo that same grunt and complete the task. Survival based on adaptation of weapons—the only change being technology.

Development of human skills with a weapon substantially contributes to the further development of that weapon. Case in point is the development of the oldest and most prevalent weapon in the history of mankind—the sword. Started as a slashing implement, it was later discovered that thrusting was superior to slashing because thrusting more effectively rendered the enemy incapacitated. Hence the development of the Gladius (ancient thrusting sword utilized by the well-trained legions of the early Roman Empire). Later on in the 15th century the development of the rapier (in Italy, Spain, and England) dominated both the European battlefields of the day as well as civilian interpersonal combat, otherwise known as duels.

The international community reflected this same pattern. In Japan the famous katana (slightly curved fighting sword) and its counterpart the wakizashi are still world renowned for their capability as formidable edged weapons. Throughout the Filipino, Malaysian and Indonesian archipelagos a similar transformation from slashing to thrusting weapons ensued. The thrusting system was superior to the slashing system and led to further edged weapons developments such as the stiletto (fully developed in Italy) and other close-quarter thrusting weapons.

Merely 150 years or so prior to the writing of this manuscript, edged weapons remained readily available and were employed in combat up to and including the American Civil War.

As time marched on the quality and effectiveness of edged weapons improved and along with this improvement was the codification and systematizing of related training systems. In Japan the art of Iaido (traditional Japanese swordsmanship) and Kendo (the art of Japanese fencing) were battlefield-dominant for centuries and critical to the complexion of geopolitical developments which forged the history of Japan. In China the ancient combative arts of Wu Shu and multiple systems of Kung Fu formed the basis of nearly all the edged weapons systems utilized by the ancient Chinese Dynasties as far back as 496 AD (first recorded reference) and no doubt prior.

In the Philippines, edged weapons systems known as "Kali," "Eskrima" and "Arnis" (among others) were instrumental in the defense and governing of the islands. In fact mid-march of the year 1521 the first national hero of the Philippines, a warrior chieftain named Lapu Lapu from Mactan (a Cebuano Island in the Visayan region) along with fellow warriors armed with spears and swords terminated the lives of famed Portuguese Captain Ferdinand Magellan and his crew in what was later identified as the "Battle of Mactan." Resistance to European colonization throughout the Malaysian, Indonesian and Philippine archipelagos was fortified by motivated and well-trained warriors in the edged weapons fighting systems they utilized.

Even in Europe where "a man must defend his honor with a sword" it required "an average of 30 hours per week for a gentleman to maintain his fighting skills" in the event he were challenged to a duel to defend his honor and in many cases his social status. As a result of this "requirement," the number of salons or sword-fighting schools that were established throughout the Elizabethan era exceeded those of the number of convenience grocery stores now found in just about any neighborhood in America.

The systems and styles of fighting in the European tradition were numerous and intricate. The skill level, similar to their Asian counterparts, was elevated to an art form. The Arte of Defence, as it was sometimes referred, dominated Western Europe and was subsequently carried throughout the globe by conquistadores, colonists and missionaries. These once-readily-available European edged weapon fighting systems today are virtually extinct. However, many of the ancient yet effective techniques and methods utilized by the warriors defending the Southeast Asian nations where these European systems were applied exist today. One can study the edged weapon arts of the Philippines or Indonesia and readily see examples of this modern-day conservation.

Drawing upon the still-extant documents and illustrations of the German ("Talhoffers Fechtbuch" circa1467), Italian ("True Arte of Defense" Giacomo DIGrassi—circa 1594), English ("Paradoxes of Defence" circa 1599), Vincentio Saviolo ("His Practise" circa 1594) as well as the direct instruction of the modern-day Arnistadores Punong Guro Edgar G. Sulite (September 25, 1957—April 10, 1997), Grand Master Leovigildo M. Giron (August 20, 1911—May 21, 2002), Guru Besar Herman Suwanda (February 10, 1955—March 23, 2000) and the conservator of more than 30 of these individual fighting systems, Guro Dan Inosanto, this material is presented to the reader for depth and understanding.

Concentrating the knowledge of the edged weapon masters of antiquity as well as the modern masters, I had the outstanding opportunity to personally train with them here in the US and at their islands of origin and also train with my teachers' teachers from whom a great majority of this material was derived.

The forthcoming material hails from this pool of knowledge presented to the reader as "roots of the tree." The masters say "Without roots the tree falls down"—that is to say without a strong foundation there is nothing upon which to build.

Given the above background, depth and history, it is my intention for the reader to take advantage of this opportunity to review the teachings of the masters in the Art of Disarming.

Scope of Study

The scope of study for this manuscript will include the fundamentals and practical application of disarming an edged weapon at extreme close quarters. "Disarming" is the taking away of a weapon from the hand or hands of your opponent. There are many different systems, there are many different methods of disarming. These are all considered "tools in the toolbox." The material covered in this manuscript is not considered <u>the</u> way, but <u>a</u> way to accomplish the task of taking a weapon away from your opponent.

An important topic to discuss in relation to disarming is the movies versus reality. What you see in the movies and what actually occurs in real life are two different things. In the movies even superstars like Jackie Chan, Chuck Norris and Jet Li require hours and hours of preparation and choreography to make a scene look right. In real life, you've only got one shot. In most cases you've got less than a second and a half. With those factors in mind, the purpose of this training is so you have something in your tool kit to use, should you need it.

When and why would you use a disarming technique? First off, if you have enough space and time to run away then this is of course the very best option as there is no need to engage your threat in any way. This is the safest option. Let's say you exercise your Constitutional right to bear arms (are carrying a firearm for personal defense) and you have the time and space (basic firearms skills and training) to access and utilize your firearm then bringing a knife to a gunfight is pretty much self-explanatory. If you have something in your hand such as a baseball bat, piece of wood or a pipe or something of this nature and you can utilize it in self-defense—again a great option. However, none of these options is what this manuscript is about.

The goal of this manuscript is to provide you with the right tool for the right job should it be the case that you have no other options available to you (no gun, no space, no time, no help) in an edged weapons altercation where you are alone, in a confined area pinned against a wall or stairway, nowhere to run, no firearm, no other options available whatsoever—a VERY worse-case scenario. The basic choices here are death or disarm.

In order to provide you with these tools, this program of instruction is divided into two equally important parts: combative concepts (software) and the actual physical techniques (hardware). Just like a computer can't run software without hardware and vice versa, so too does successful understanding and eventual sustainment of the material in this manuscript depend upon understanding both the combative concepts and physical techniques.

Let's start with the software.

PART 1
COMBATIVE CONCEPTS

RANGES OF ENGAGEMENT

There are two ranges of engagement that we're going to look at. The first one is "non-contact range." In this range, you have plenty of space between you and the attacker, the knife attack is occurring at a distance which gives you time and space to make decisions and to basically get out of the situation. That's not what this training is all about. This training is about the other range of engagement: "contact range." You're stuck in a confined area of operation, maybe in a corner, against a wall, you're backed up and there's no way you can get out. Remember you have no gun, no other options. Basically, when he's coming at you at this range, you have two options, you can stand there and take it like a man (less than optimal) or you can go into one of the techniques we're going to look at in this manuscript.

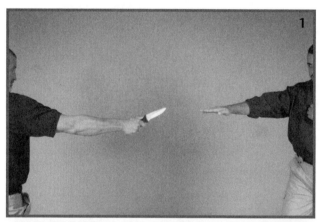

At non-contact range, as displayed here, there is enough room between you and your attacker that you can choose the safest option— RUN! Increased space allows for more decision making time.

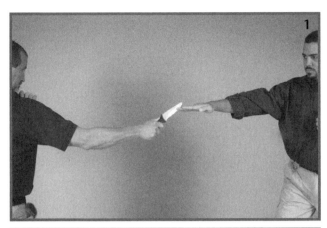

Contact range, as displayed here, is the range where an attacker can already make contact with any part of your body. With reduced space, there is less time for decision making, the fight could be on quicker than you think.

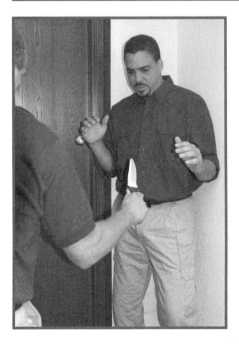

Here is a "real world" depiction of contact range. Backed into a corner, there is no room to escape. The defender's choices are extremely limited.

REACTIONARY GAP

A second key concept is the Reactionary Gap. As discussed above, more space allows for more reaction time and therefore, more options. The reactionary gap refers to the increased or diminished reaction time allowed by the distance between two people, and is illustrated in the two pictures below. On the left there is enough space between the two men for the tossed ball not to surprise its catcher. On the right the distance between the two men is shortened giving the catcher less margin for error.

SCALE OF INJURY

Related to the Reactionary Gap is the Scale of Injury. This is a method for defining the risk of personal injury in an interpersonal conflict scenario. Essentially, the farther you are from the attacker the lower your risk of injury (more space equals more reaction time), and the closer you are, the greater your risk. As the pictures below show, at non-contact range there is no contact so there is no injury. As the two parties move closer, the risk of injury increases from a minor hand cut (band aid), to deeper muscle tissue cut (recoverable injury), to limb loss or paralysis (unrecoverable injury), to the worst case scenario: death.

The scale of injury is essential for understanding the relationship your distance from an attacker has to your safety.

This sequence of photos shows the Scale of Injury from no injury to worst case scenario: death.

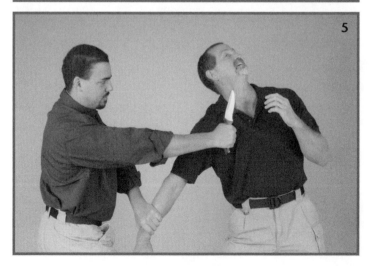

Safe and Unsafe Positions

Naturally the positional possibilities for two people to be in relation to one another are countless, so for simplicity we will break those possibilities down to two basic positions—a safe zone (referred to as the Green Zone) and an unsafe zone (Red Zone). The term Red Zone refers to that position where you are in front of your attacker and are at great risk of being hit with impact, edged or personal weapons (fist, elbow, etc). The term Green Zone refers to that position outside your attacker's arms or behind him, thereby making it more difficult for your attacker to hit you, and easier for you to control your attacker and consequently the fight.

Here are two examples of the Green Zone, one at non-contact range, the other behind the attacker's back.

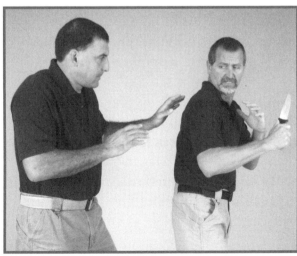

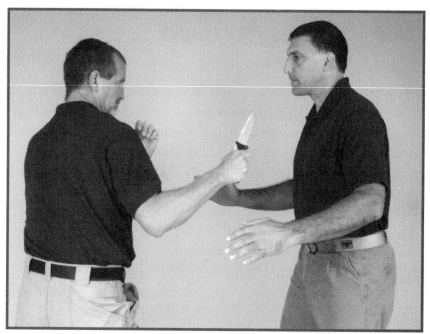

*Above is an example of the Red Zone. Directly in front
of your attacker is the worst place to be.*

EXIT OR EQUALIZE

One of the most important combative concepts is "exit or equal-ize." These are your two options at non-contact range. When a threat presents itself, you certainly don't want to put your hands in the meat grinder, the safest thing to do is get yourself out of there, also known as "exit."

The other option is "equalize." That is, use an item in your hands like a bag or something nearby like a garbage can lid that you can put between yourself and the threat. Then, while facing the threat, equalize it momentarily by throwing the item at your attacker and then exit. Keep in mind that plenty of space is also something that you can place between yourself and your attacker.

ACTION VS. REACTION

You should only utilize a disarming technique if there are no other options whatsoever. If it's a situation where you are stuck, nowhere to move, no possibility of exit or nothing with which to momentarily equalize the situation, that's the only place a disarm should be applied.

Another key point in understanding the application of a disarming technique is what's called "action/reaction" or some people call it the "action/reaction power curve." If I'm in a situation where there's a potential threat that presents itself and I see the threat, I then react to it. My attacker has taken action, I now need to react. Perhaps I step off the line of attack. I have reacted to his action, I'm behind the power curve. By taking that step off the line of attack, I have forced him behind the power curve because now he needs to react to my action.

The whole concept here is to work to always be ahead of that power curve. When you're taking action, he's reacting, the more you can do this the more you will take control of the fight. If he's acting and you're reacting, he takes control of the fight. This is not the desired situation. The goal here is for you to take control of the fight. You take action and remain in control of the fight by taking control of the action/reaction power curve.

TIMING

If we move into contact range, when the attack comes in, the distance between the blade and a vital part of the body is zero. The scale of injury is very high at this range. One of the most important components of disarming is timing. *When* you apply the technique is the key to solving problems. If I apply the technique *before* the attack, it's too early. If I apply the technique *after* the attack, it's too late.

This is similar to driving up to a traffic light. Stopping too soon, at a green light for example, can cause just as many problems as continuing to move through the red light. Most of us try and time the yellow light by adjusting placement of our vehicle based on the timing of the light. Same concept applies for application of any disarming technique. The technique has to be applied exactly on time, which means timing the attack to the target and intersecting it exactly half way between his centerline and your centerline.

In summary, you have three elements of timing: before, during and after. The entirety of the material in this manuscript will deal with the placement of that technique *during* the attack.

ACCIDENTAL OR INCIDENTAL

In training with the masters over the years, there was a phrase that they used that was associated with disarming, and that is, "All disarms are either accidental or incidental." An example of "accidental" would be, the attack comes in and I put my hands up to defend myself and just by accident my elbow happens to nail the attacker's hand and the blade comes loose from his grip. There was no intention, just accidentally my elbow happened to hit his hand and the blade fell out.

"Incidental" means the disarm was done "with purpose." I block his attack and notice there is an opportunity for a disarming technique, so I take advantage of that rare opportunity and apply a pragmatic disarming technique.

A clear example of an accidental disarm would be if you were carrying a book in your hand while walking and accidentally your hand hits an unseen object like a trash can, door knob or counter top and knocks the object out of your hand. What happens in this example is the unexpected impact your hand makes with the unseen immovable object loosens your grip on whatever it is you are holding. That accidental impact could also be seen as a strike to the hand. The same thing applies to an incoming weapon. A hand is a common human appendage predominantly utilized for grasping. The hand can hold a book, it can hold a cup of coffee, it has an opposing digit (which we'll look at a little bit later in our training), so if the attack comes in and you strike the attacker's weapon hand, this is one of the most effective methods to release the grip on whatever might be in the hand.

STRIKE OR CONTROL

There are two combative concepts that go together with this idea: *strike* or *control* the weapon hand. In the previous example we saw the use of striking the weapon hand. The other option is to *control* the weapon hand or arm. For example, if we take a look at the incoming attack, the first response was to strike the weapon hand or weapon arm (whether it's with your elbow, hand, screwdriver, hammer, you name it). Our second option of controlling the weapon hand or arm can be accomplished by firmly holding on to the attacker's weapon side wrist and elbow, or have both your hands on the wrist or elbow.

To reiterate, our combative concept here is either *strike* or *control* the weapon arm. We haven't really discussed any technique yet, we've only worked with what we call combative concepts. We're going to stay on the concepts for just a little bit longer, but speaking of technique, during my entire career as a full time instructor in the professional training community, many questions came up about the art of disarming. They were really the impetus for the creation of this program of instruction. One of the most common questions over the years has been, "What's the one technique that will work every single time?" Well, there's no such thing. Silver bullets are a work of fiction. There is no single technique that will work every time, because if there was, we'd all know what it was and we wouldn't need to have this type of training.

Technique is a highly subjective matter, and we're really not going to focus on one technique for one particular attack. What we're really going to do is take a series of attacks and utilize what is statistically the most probable series of techniques that can be applied to that series of attacks. That's not very specific, but it will give you the best possible option as a tool in your toolbox to apply a disarming technique against an incoming, aggressive, edged weapon attack.

Sometimes this can be a difficult concept to grasp. We can once again liken this to a driving scenario. Let's say you're driving your car on a highway traveling at about 60 MPH. All of a sudden someone cuts you off. What exact driving technique will you use to avoid a collision? Will your turn sharply to the right? Turn sharply to the left? Apply the breaks? Accelerate? Perhaps some combination thereof? Why can't you tell me exactly what technique you would use in that scenario? The answer is that no two scenarios are the same. Throughout the remainder of this training manuscript we will address what can be considered the disarming training equivalent to usage of the steering wheel, the brakes and the gas pedal in reference to our driving analogy of immediate response to a knife attack.

In the same context, especially in the professional training environment, a lot of "what if" questions came up such as, "What if a team of ninjas dressed in black rappelled into the room through the ceiling with fully automatic weapons?" It's undeniably a "what if," but it's not realistic. So we're going to keep the "what ifs" to practical application, and not go too far off the handle with such scenarios.

RETURN, RELEASE, RETAIN

Last but certainly not least of our combative concepts is the concept of "Return, Release, and Retain." What do we mean by that? Ask any cop out there, he'll tell you it's the hands that kill. If the opponent has something in his hands, he can hurt you or possibly kill you with it. Very much worth repeating—It's the hands that kill.

The whole disarming concept here is control of the weapon hand and/or control of the weapon arm. Manipulation and control of the weapon arm and/or hand is the key to success in any disarming technique. The old saying "control that which is wielding the weapon and you control the weapon" directly applies to the art of disarming.

So how does this apply? *How* do we control? *How* do we manipulate? There are three methods of manipulating or controlling the weapon hand or weapon arm. They are: *Return*, meaning to return the weapon back to the attacker—a method that is recommended for beginning students; *Release*, meaning to release the weapon completely from the hand of the attacker—recommended for intermediate students; or *Retain*, meaning you are able to retain the weapon from the hand of the attacker. Retaining the weapon requires the highest degree of skill possible and is not recommended for anyone but the most advanced and senior student of the art of disarming. Consequently, these are structured in such a manner as the easiest is first, and the most difficult is last. It's easier to return, a little more difficult to release and most difficult to retain a weapon you have taken away from your opponent. Again, *return, release, and retain*; these are the three possibilities of controlling or manipulating the weapon arm.

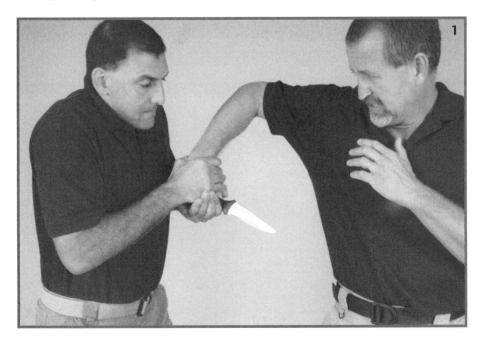

An example of defending yourself from an edged weapon attack and returning the blade to the attacker.

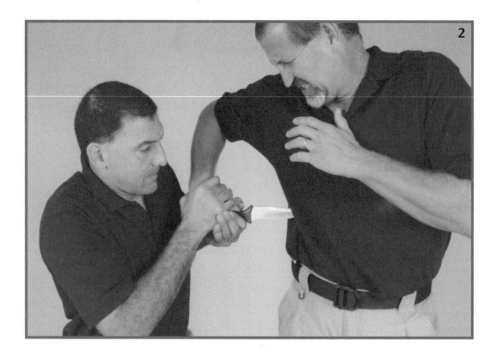

An example of defending yourself against an edged weapon attack and releasing the blade from the attacker's grip.

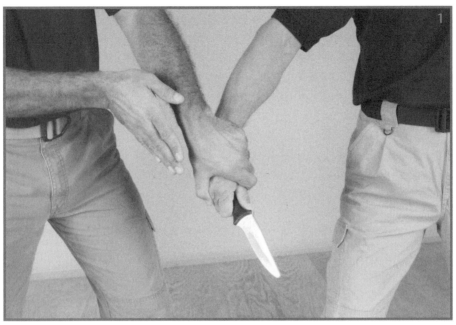

This series shows one method of retaining the attacker's weapon after successfully defending oneself against an edged weapon attack.

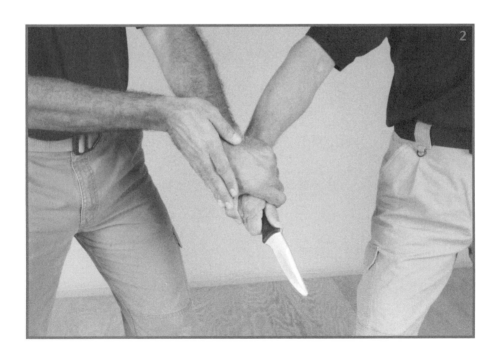

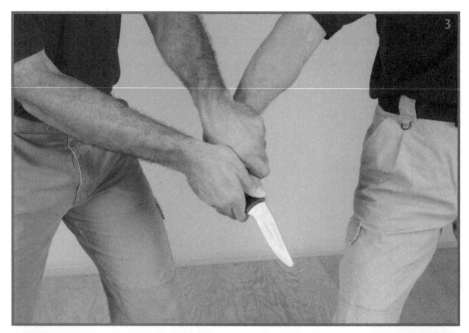

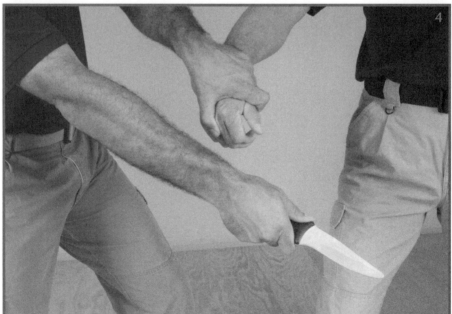

This concludes our first block of training: *combative concepts.*
Our remaining blocks of training focus on the actual practical application, applying these combative concepts in disarming techniques.
So let's start our physical training.

PART II
PHYSICAL TRAINING

STABLE FIGHTING PLATFORM

The fundamentals of physical training start from establishing a stable base from which to deliver a disarming technique. This is commonly referred to as a "stable fighting platform." How do we build a stable fighting platform from which to deliver these disarming techniques? Very simply, from the ground up. Starting with the feet about shoulder width apart, firmly planted allowing you a stable base of operation, toes facing toward the threat, knees slightly bent like a spring, ready to move in any direction. The hips should be placed directly over the feet to allow maximum stability. The hands should obviously be above the waist to provide maximum protection for the head and neck. If you combine the hands, which are above the belt, and the feet, which are in a stable position, the combination of these hands and feet is what establishes a stable fighting platform.

The Stable Fighting Platform: hands above the waist, knees bent, feet shoulder width and toes facing the threat.

Knowing that a stable fighting platform will allow optimal delivery of a disarming technique, we have to weigh that against the known fact that a stationary target is easier to hit than a moving target. Since a moving target is harder to hit, it would be optimal if we could move this stable fighting platform from one position to another.

MOVING THE STABLE FIGHTING PLATFORM

There are various methods for moving the stable fighting platform. We can move the stable fighting platform forward by taking the lead leg and moving it forward touching heel first then toe then sliding the rear leg along. We can move it backward by taking the rear leg and moving it backward toe then heel and sliding the lead leg along.

We can also move laterally in both directions. If you are moving to the left, be sure to move your left leg first and slide your right leg second. Vice versa for moving to the right, move your right leg first and slide your left leg second. Be certain not to cross your legs.

The main reason for all of this movement is that a moving target is more difficult to hit than a stationary one. Remember our application, we're stuck, we're in a confined area of operation. There's not going to be a lot of movement if we're applying a disarming technique. If there was, then we'd go back to step one which was the safest: exit or equalize.

If, in fact, you are attacked in a confined area of operation, it's necessary for you to turn and face the threat. There are two methods to accomplish this. You can either take the lead leg and turn and face the threat in a manner that moves *towards* the threat. Or if you don't have any room to turn and face, you may have to step back, so you can do a quarter turn pivot by stepping *back* and facing the threat. Those two options again are, step *towards* the threat, or step *back* from the threat using whatever minimal space you may have in this confined area of operation.

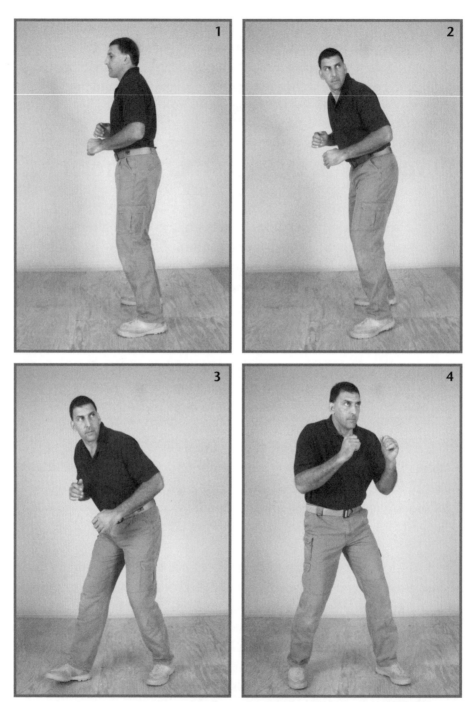

Moving the SFP. The SFP can be employed from any position
in which the body may be situated. In this example, the defender
observes a threat to his left and turns into the threat to face it.

Distract, Disable, Disarm

One of the most common misconceptions regarding the art of disarming is that a well-trained person can simply remove any weapon from the hand of his adversary at will. This is simply not true. We can compare this to a professional basketball player—well trained to place the ball into the basket. However, can he always complete this task at will? At the free-throw line? With opposing team members defending? The same applies to disarming—it cannot be accomplished "at will" as there are many factors involved.

Using the basketball analogy, a player must first outmaneuver his opponent, place him off-balance, at a disadvantage. It is *only* while his opponent is trying to recover (catch up to the action/reaction power curve) that our professional player can attempt to complete his task of sinking that basket.

The same exact set of circumstances applies to an altercation with an edged weapon. Your opponent must be outmaneuvered, placed off balance and at a disadvantage in order to allow for application of a disarming technique. How does one accomplish this task of outmaneuvering, placing your opponent off balance and at a disadvantage?

There are a couple tools in the toolbox made available to accomplish these tasks. These are distracting and disabling your opponent prior to disarming him. A handy way to remember this is the "Three D's"—Distract, Disable, Disarm.

Getting him to think of something else—that is force his attention from his initial assault on you (offense) and place it on his own personal safety (defense) is a sufficient enough distraction. Disabling is simply a matter of negatively impacting his handling of the weapon he is holding (in this case an edged weapon).

There are countless methods for distracting your opponent from his intended attack. Here are some examples.

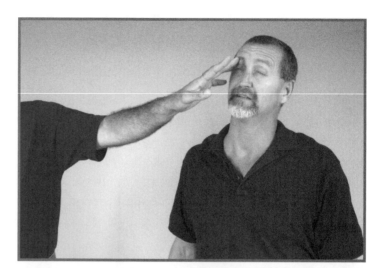

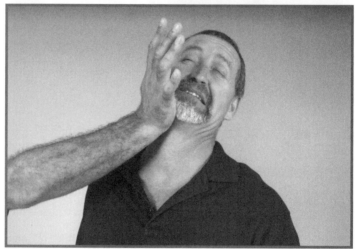

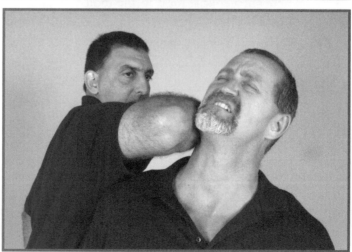

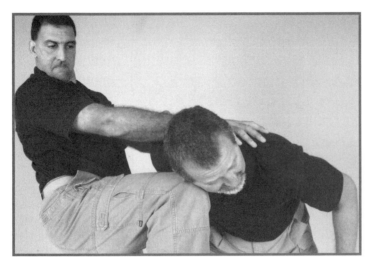

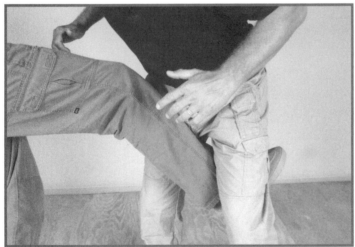

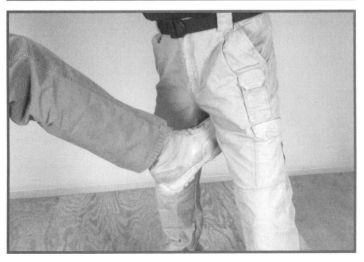

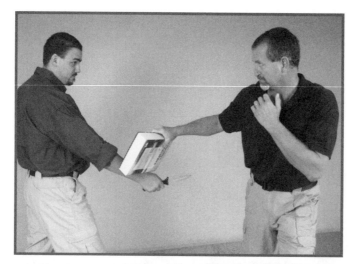

Limiting the risk of physical injury, here are some examples of the defender assisting his disabling technique with a hand-held implement.

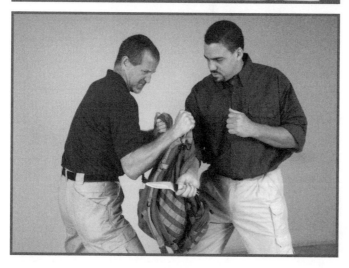

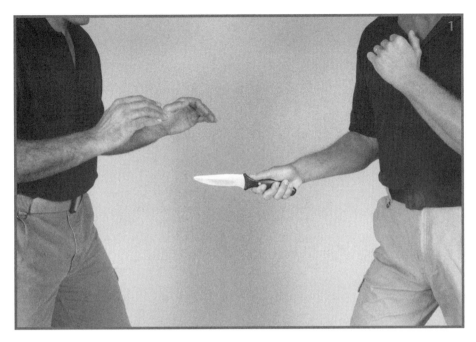

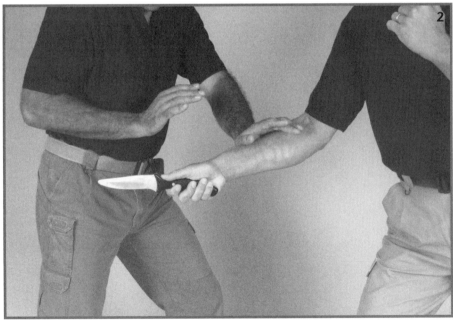

*Defending a low line thrusting attack, the defender
utilizes his hands to disable the incoming attack.*

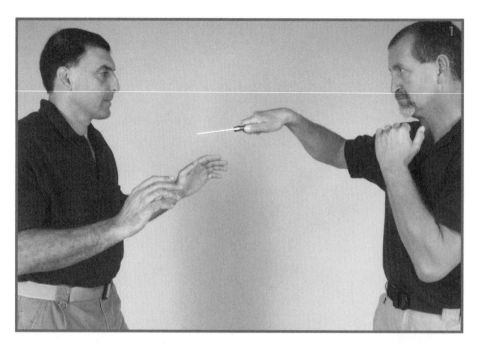

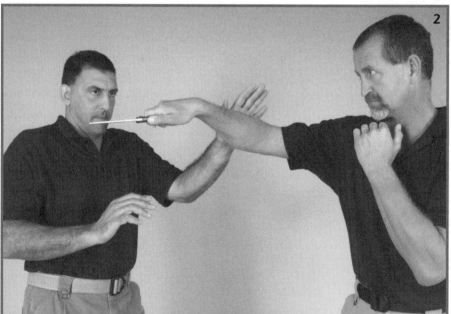

*Defending a high line thrusting attack, the defender
utilizes his hands to disable the incoming attack.*

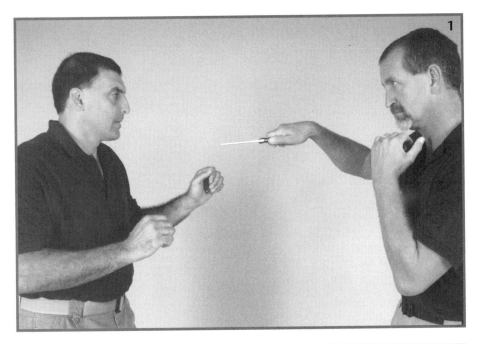

Defending a high line thrusting attack, the defender utilizes his forearms to disable the incoming attack.

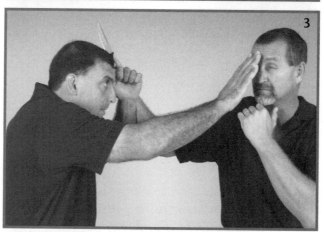

Defending a high line forehand slashing attack, the defender
utilizes his forearms to disable the incoming attack and
adds a finger jab distraction to the attacker's eyes.

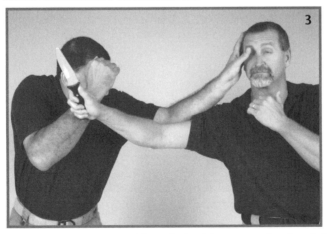

*Defending a high line backhand slashing attack, the defender
utilizes his forearms to disable the incoming attack and
adds a finger jab distraction to the attacker's eyes.*

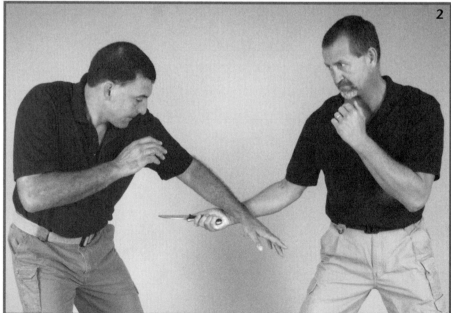

*Defending a low line forehand slashing attack, the defender
utilizes his forearm to disable the incoming attack.*

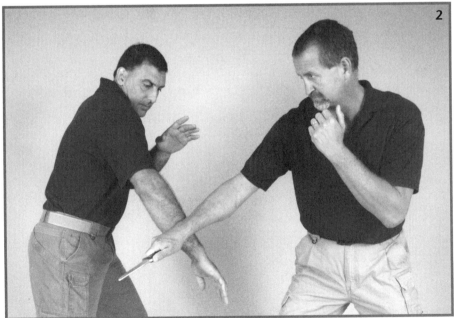

Defending a low line backhand slashing attack, the defender utilizes his forearm to disable the incoming attack.

FATHER OF THE FOUR FINGERS

One of my instructors, Punonguro Edgar Sulite (now deceased), founded the Lameco System of Eskrima, one of the arts that has a very high level of proficiency at disarming. One of the things he shared with me was the concept of the "father of the four fingers." He considered the thumb, our opposing digit, to be the father of the four fingers, and he used to say to me, "Stib (Filipino for Steve), if you can control the thumb, you can control the whole hand." So the meat and potatoes of disarming any weapon is positive control of the thumb.

The basic concept here is to take the strongest part of your hand, which is the four fingers opposing the thumb, and place those fingers on the base of your opponent's thumb. Not on the thumbnail, not on the wrist, but on the base of the thumb. If you can control the small muscle at the base of the thumb which activates the thumb, you can control the weapon, and if you control the father of the four fingers, you control the hand.

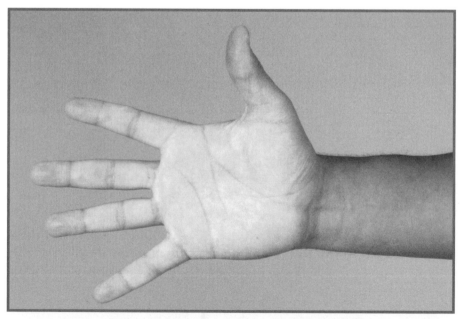

The "father of the four fingers" is the thumb, our opposing digit.

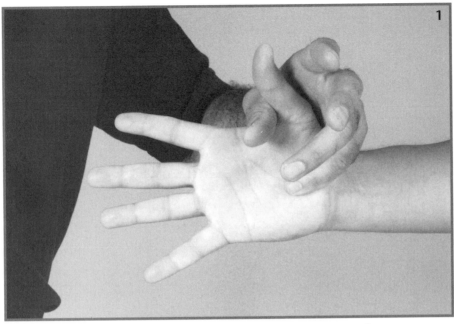

*Utilizing the strongest part of your grip, the four fingers,
control your attacker's thumb in order to control his hand
and therefore his grip on his weapon. In this sequence
of pictures your grip is acquired from the side.*

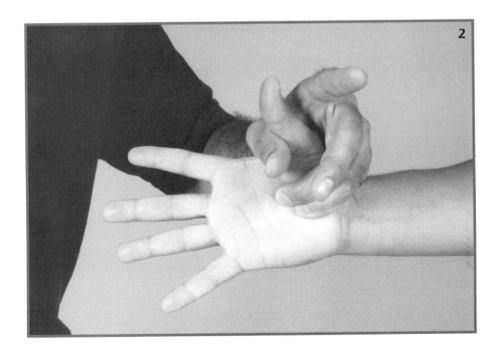

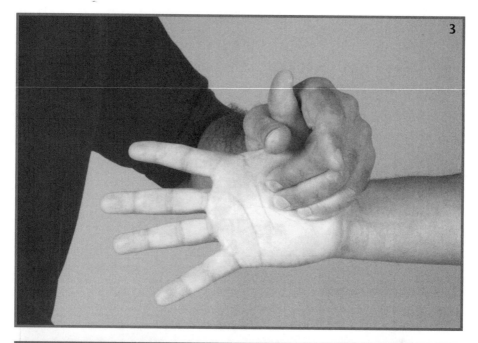

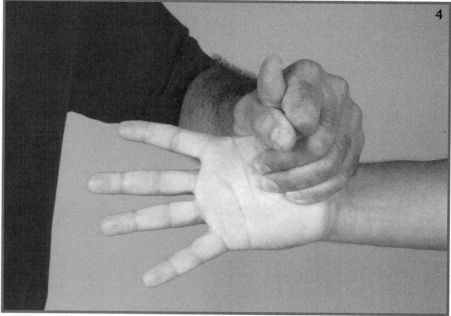

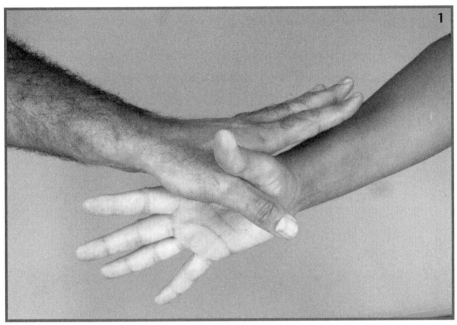

Still utilizing your fingers to control your attacker's thumb, these photos show acquiring the grip from above your attacker's hand.

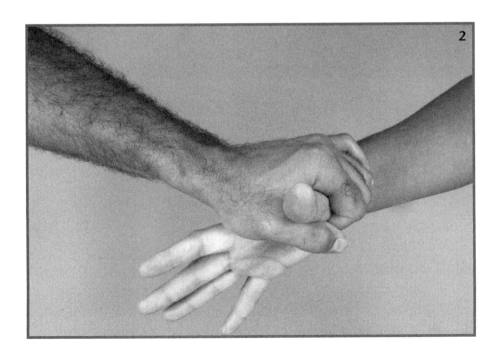

Another important element passed on to us by the masters is the concept of "keeping safe." There are two pieces to that puzzle, especially with an edged weapon. First you must *make safe your body*, and then you can *make safe the weapon*. This does two things for you, it puts space between you and the actual weapon itself, and it moves you to a position of advantage outside your attacker's weapon arm, considered a *position of dominance* in some schools. If you recall our earlier block of training on *Exit or Equalize,* the best of these is to not have your body anywhere near the path of the incoming blade.

To counter an edged weapon attack, you must first make safe your body. In this example the defender steps off the line of attack using his hand to simultaneously deflect the attacker's weapon arm.

The defender now uses his forearm to deflect the incoming attack. Utilization of this technique might be because the defender was caught with his hands low. At contact range there would not be enough time to employ the hand so he uses the most efficient tool at his disposal, in this case the forearm. Make safe the weapon.

We're going to focus our studies on two types of attacks: the thrust and the slash. A thrust can be to the low line, about belt level, and a thrust can also be to the high line, for example a straight line thrust to the throat area. The other type of attack is a slash. A slash can also come in from the high line or low line.

Although both of these attacks can be devastating and life threatening, each deserves a little more detail. In ancient times, about the era of formation of the vast armies of the Roman Empire, just before they were formed into the famed Roman Legions, there were individuals called military chroniclers. These individuals were employed by the Romans to write down what they observed in battle. In ancient times, believe it or not, the very early Roman army used to employ a curved, slashing type of weapon. During usage of this slashing weapon, the chroniclers observed the enemy often fell down, but got back up and continued fighting. When the troops used a thrusting motion, it was observed and recorded that the enemy would go down and stay down.

After the battle in the after action reports of the day, the generals made note that when the troops employed the thrust, the enemy went down and stayed down, when the troops employed the slash, the enemy went down but most of the time got up again. So they decided to have all the troops only use thrusting attacks and when the next battle came up, the chroniclers observed that the usage of the thrust increased the kill ratio by about 90 per cent, proving that thrusting was superior to slashing with regards to felling an enemy. Later it caused the armies of the day to change to a sword that was designed primarily for thrusting, known as the *gladius*.

Time passed and around the middle of the 16th century, European duelists such as Giacomo DiGrassi (Italy) and George Silver (Great Britain) wrote manuscripts of their duels. Being the experts of the day at hand to hand combat with edged weapons, their writings show that they also considered a thrust to be superior to a slash. In fact, a thrust about four inches deep was determined to be enough to terminate human life. Ironically, this is the primary cause for the majority of the fifty United States to set the "legal length" of a concealed carry knife to less than four inches.

In our modern times, people who work in emergency rooms have also discovered that a thrust, with a screwdriver or shank or edged weapon, causes more damage than a slash. So history, as well as contemporary observation, demonstrates that the thrust poses more of a threat to loss of life than the slash. So with that in mind we're going to focus our training primarily on the thrust. We will later cover some aspects of handling a slashing attack, but right now we're going to focus on the thrust.

With regards to delivering a thrust, the human hand can be placed in three positions. The palm can be facing upward, downward or the palm can be vertical. All three of those palm positions can result in a successful forward motion known as a thrust.

From the palm up position, a very simple forward movement results in a thrust toward the midsection. The palm can be vertical, facilitating the same type of attack and palm down as well. These are the three palm positions that we're going to work with for the remainder of our training.

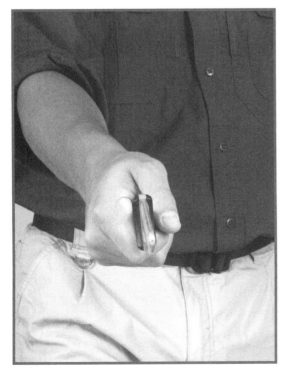

Knife grip in the vertical palm configuration.

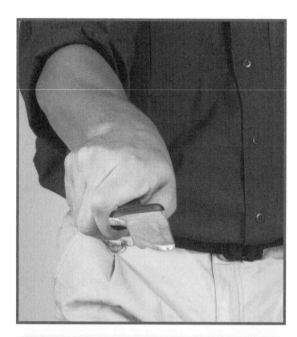

Knife grip in the palm down configuration.

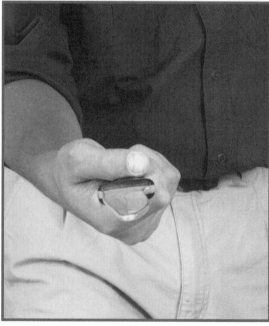

Knife grip in the palm up configuration.

Going back to our three methods of disarming: *return* to sender, *release* the weapon from your opponent's hand, and *retaining* the weapon after taking it from your opponent's hand, we're going to focus this next section on *return to sender*.

HANDS THAT KILL

Remember, it's the hands that kill. It's something he's holding in his hand that will cause damage to your body. The weakest part of the weapon arm, the weakest link in the chain, is the wrist. The arm is full of powerful muscles: strong shoulders, biceps, and forearms, the weakest part of the weapon arm is the wrist.

The tiny muscle that we described earlier is the thumb. Remember controlling the thumb means you're controlling the father of the four fingers. Our focus on this section of our training is the "return to sender." What is it exactly that we're returning to the sender? The weapon, of course, but really the main factor here is the palm. The key to this section is, "Where is the palm facing?" Remember we had three hand positions; we want to return the palm of the hand back to the sender. So we're going to push the palm in some way to place it as close as we can to the center line of the attacker. This is the essence of return to sender: the *redirection of the palm*.

We're going to start with our first series of return to sender techniques based on defending a thrusting attack. But before we do that, let's take a look at the anatomy of a thrust so we can properly defend against it. Very similar to the military that examines an enemy's aircraft or an enemy's submarines so that they can better defend against those technologies, we're going to do the same thing here with an analysis of the anatomy of a thrust defense.

The most important questions regarding a thrust defense is how can a thrust come toward your vital organs? The thrust can be delivered on the low line, meaning just above the belt; the thrust can be delivered on the high line to the upper chest and throat. The thrust can be straight or it can be curved. Also, the angle or line of delivery can vary. It can be angled vertically up, horizontal, vertically down, etc.

So we have to worry about these three things: Is it a low line attack? Is it a high line attack? Is it a straight line attack? Is it a curved attack? And lastly, what direction is the thrust coming from? What is the angle or line of attack?

We've looked at distracting and disabling, in this next physical training section, we're going to focus on the disarming techniques themselves. It is essential to remember these techniques are for when your back is against the wall (figuratively or literally) and you have no choice but to go hands on versus an attacker armed with an edged weapon. Regarding interpersonal human conflict with an edged weapon at close quarters (you are pinned up against a wall with a knife to your throat or belly with no where to run and completely out of options) is very ugly business. It doesn't get much worse than this with regards to an individual attack with edged weapons, so I cannot stress enough the need for you to truly be out of options before facing an armed attacker without a weapon of your own. First question that comes to mind is "What about multiple attackers?" Well, unfortunately you're already behind the power curve even with one assailant and although there are certain techniques available, the scope of study for this manuscript will be purposely focused on single attacker only.

The thrust is considered one of the most dangerous attacks and, of course, a majority of our training will be allocated to handling this type of attack, however, there are also various slashes—forehand and backhand which if applied to the appropriate body part could render the victim severely injured or possibly dead.

Throughout the upcoming training, techniques to defend against both the devastating thrust and forehand and backhand slash attacks with an edged weapon will be addressed. Whether defending against a thrust or a slash and regardless of if it may be a high-line or low-line or mid-line attack, we'll group these disarming techniques into the three categories as covered above: Return, Release and Retain.

PART III
RETURN

As covered earlier there are three primary disarming responses available to the defender—to **return** the weapon hand (and weapon) to the sender, to **release** the weapon from the attacker's hand and lastly to remove the weapon from your attacker's grip and **retain** it in your hand to utilize in a manner that you determine to be an appropriate response option. The least complex of these last-ditch defense responses is the RETURN option so we'll start with that one.

Let's keep in mind the basics—make safe the body and then make safe the weapon, the three D's (Distract, Disable and Disarm), father of the four fingers, etc. Remember, you are trapped up against a wall in a confined area by an aggressive and violent attacker intent on extinguishing your lights. In this situation and with nowhere to run and nothing in your hands (failing Exit or Equalize) there are only two remaining options at your disposal—apply some type of defense (disarming technique) or just stand there and get cut open or stabbed to death.

Return to sender #1:

With the attack coming in at contact range, immediately step off the line of attack (make safe your body) and utilize your support side hand to disable the incoming thrust attack.

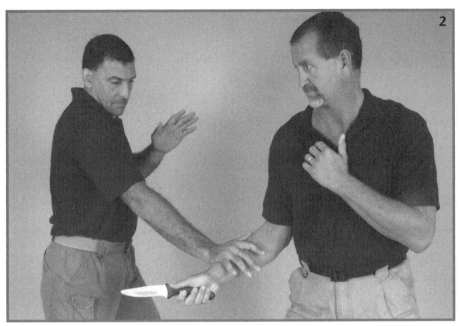

*Angle the incoming attack down and away
with your strong side hand.*

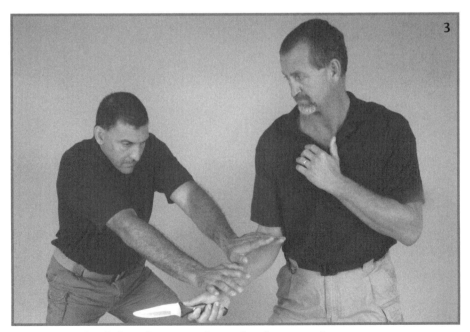

*Use both hands to continue the down and away pressure
while simultaneously bending at the hips to gain space
between your body and the attacker's weapon.*

With your strong side hand controlling the father of the
four fingers (the attacker's thumb) and your support side
hand cupping the back of the attacker's hand, bend his
wrist and start forcing his palm toward his body.

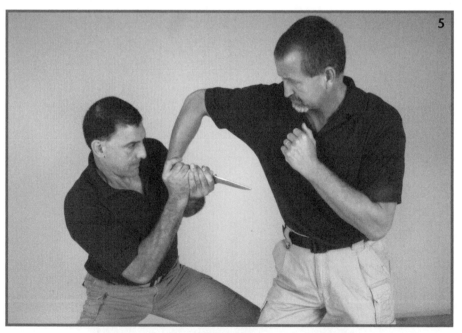

Lower your base to increase your leverage
and return the attacker's blade to sender.

Return to sender #2:

The attacker is already at contact range. Immediate defensive action must be taken in this life and death encounter.

Step off the line of attack as you disable the incoming attack with your support side hand.

Utilize a distraction strike to the eyes.

Use your strong side hand to control your attacker's weapon hand thumb, your support hand continues to monitor the attacker's forearm.

Maintain your strong side grip on the attacker's weapon side thumb and now utilize your support side hand to cup the back of the attacker's weapon hand.

Lower your base to increase your leverage and return the attacker's blade to sender.

Return to sender #3:

Similar to the second technique, rather than using the support side hand, this sequence utilizes the support side forearm to disable the incoming attack as well as provide the additional leverage to complete the technique.

Return to sender #4:

Defender is at contact range with an incoming backhand
attack with the blade in the point down configuration.

Use the outside of both forearms to disable
the incoming thrusting attack.

3 Control the attacker's knife hand with your strong side hand while simultaneously distracting him with a defensive eye thrust.

4 Maintain your strong side grip while you bring your support side hand to give additional control of the attacker's weapon hand and start to point the blade back toward him.

5 Continue aiming the blade at the attacker as you complete the return to sender.

Return to sender #5:

Once again at contact range with no other choice but to engage,
the defender is faced with a forehand thrusting attack with
the knife in the point down configuration.

Utilize your support side hand to disable
the incoming attack.

Use your support side forearm and strong side hand to guide the attacker's blade across your center line and away from your body.

Use both hands to control the attacker's knife arm.

Return the blade to sender into the attacker's hip line.

Return the blade to sender into the attacker's mid-section.

Return to sender #6:

The defender is faced with a high line forehand thrusting attack.

Disable the incoming thrusting attack by utilizing your support side hand to check the attacker's knife arm.

Distract the attacker with a defensive eye strike with your strong side hand.

Use both hands to control the attacker's knife arm.

Maintaining your strong side hand on the thumb of the attacker's knife hand use your support side forearm to assist in completing the return to sender.

Drop your base and complete the return to sender technique to the attacker's mid-section.

Return to sender #7:

Faced again at contact range with an imminent edged weapon attack and no time or space to get away the defender must mount an effective defense.

Disable the incoming forehand, standard grip slashing attack by closing the distance and keeping your hands and forearms high to protect your head and neck.

*Maintain your support side hand in a defensive position
while you distract the attacker with an eye attack
with your strong side hand.*

*Use your strong side arm underneath the attacker's
knife arm to bring his weapon outside your strong side
and get yourself to the green zone.*

Control the attacker's knife hand thumb with your strong side hand and utilize another eye attack distraction.

Maintain your strong hand grip and add your support hand to double your control on the attacker's knife hand.

*Lower your base and complete your defense
with the return to sender.*

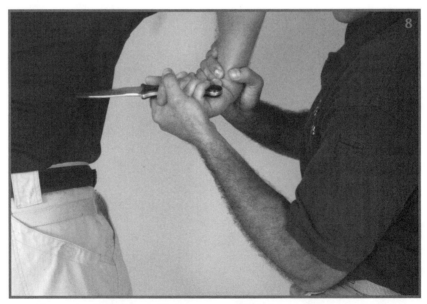

*Close up shot from the reverse angle shows the proper grip
and hand placement for maximum control
of the attacker's weapon hand.*

Return to sender #8:

At contact range with no time or space to get away, the defender prepares for a backhand, standard grip, slashing attack.

Once again, closing the distance, the defender keeps his hands and forearms high to protect his head and neck, disabling the incoming attack. He exposes only the outside of the forearms rather than the more sensitive inner part.

3 While the strong side hand controls the weapon hand, the support side hand applies an eye strike distraction.

4 Maintain your strong hand grip and add your support hand to double your control on the attacker's knife hand.

5 Lower your base and complete your defense with the return to sender.

Return to sender #9:

*At contact range with no time or space to get away,
the defender prepares to deal with a forehand,
standard grip, low line thrusting attack.*

*The defender simultaneously disables the incoming
attack with his support side hand while the strong
side hand applies an eye strike distraction.*

*The strong side hand comes down to control
the attacker's knife hand.*

*Using both hands to double the defender's control of the attacker's
knife hand, he applies a wrist lock that forces the attacker to bend
forward and makes the blade point toward the ceiling.*

With the attacker still bent forward, the defender completes the defensive return to sender technique.

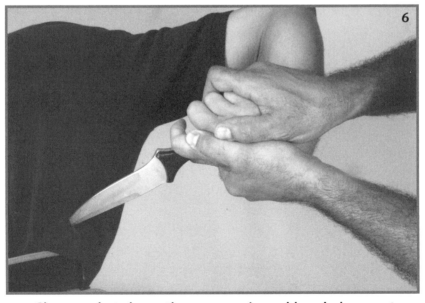

Close up shot shows the proper grip and hand placement for maximum control of the attacker's knife hand.

Return to sender #10:

At contact range with no time or space to get away, the defender prepares to deal with a backhand, standard grip, low line slashing attack.

The defender simultaneously disables the incoming attack with his strong side hand while using an eye strike with his support side hand to distract the attacker.

Maintaining contact with his strong side hand, the defender's support side hand comes over and controls the attacker's thumb of his knife hand.

Maintaining his support side grip on the attacker's knife hand, the defender aligns his strong side hand to aid in completing the technique.

*With both hands now on the attacker's knife hand
allowing for maximum control, the defender completes
the defensive return to sender technique.*

PART IV
RELEASE

Now that we've covered the *Return to Sender* component of our training it's important that the student of disarming techniques execute a substantial number of repetitions in order to engrain the new physical movements. In most training systems it would take anywhere from three to five years just working on the Return component prior to moving on the next section. It is the advice of the masters that "repetition is the mother of all skills." Please keep in mind that a very high level of proficiency is needed to complete the prior section of study before moving forward to this one.

In this intermediate segment of our training we will address the most common responses to an incoming edged weapon attack with the purpose of utilizing a *Release* response option (again, either *accidental or incidental*) disarming technique.

Again, as we move into this intermediate set of training skills, please keep in mind the basics of making safe your body and making safe the weapon, distract, disable and disarm as you have no other option except to bleed out or attempt some last ditch effort to defend against this violent personal assault.

Release #1:

You're already in a bad situation at contact range against an attacker with an edged weapon. It's too late to run. Taking it like a man is not an option; you've got to respond with appropriate technique and violence of action.

*As the thrust comes is delivered you are successfully
able to grab your attacker's weapon arm.*

*The attacker in turn grabs your arm minimizing
your ability to defend yourself.*

Circling your hand to the inside while simultaneously dropping your hips and elbow releases his grip on your arm.

Complete the circling motion with your arm vertical as you move your attacker's weapon hand across your center line.

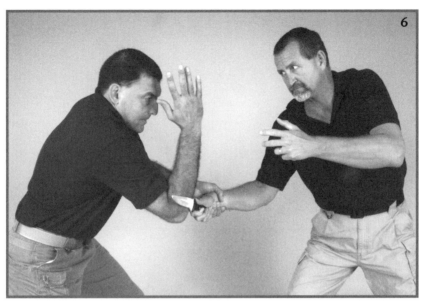

Maintain control of your attacker's weapon hand and place the outside of your forearm against the flat of your attacker's blade.

Push your forearm against the flat of the blade (forward) as you pull your attacker's hand in the exact opposite direction thereby ejecting the blade from his grip.

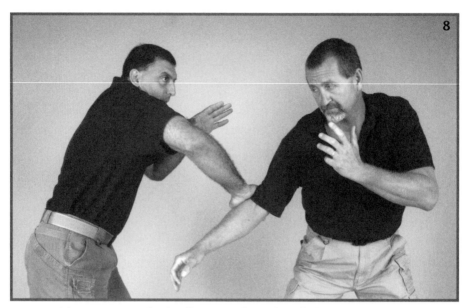

*Cup your attacker's elbow and angle off the line of attack
and away from him getting further into the
green zone outside his arm.*

*Continue pushing his arm away as you line up an
eye gouge with the thumb of your other hand.*

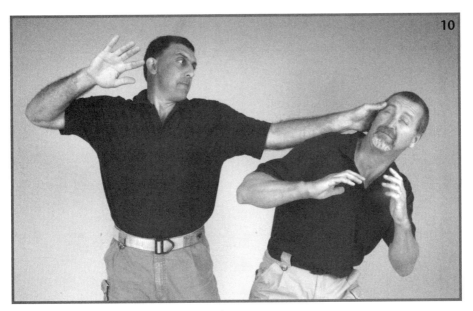

*As you execute the eye gouge, prepare
a finishing elbow with the other arm.*

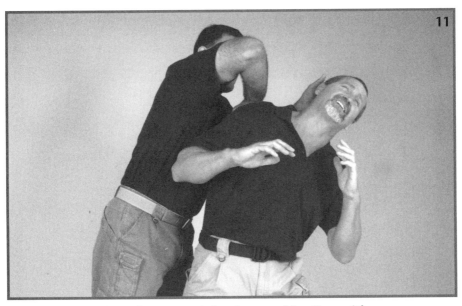

*Complete your defensive combination with
an elbow to your attacker's head.*

Release #2:

The defender is at contact range with no time or space to get
away from an imminent reverse grip, high line thrusting attack.

The defender disables the incoming attack by grabbing
the attacker's knife arm with his support side hand.

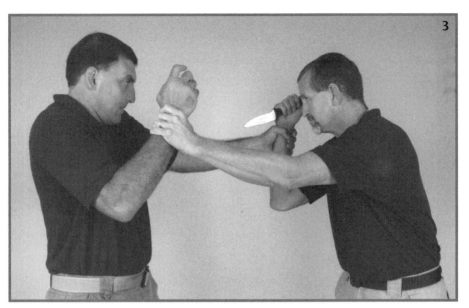

*The attacker grabs the defender's strong side
hand with his empty, support side hand.*

*The defender pushes the attacker's knife hand
across the attacker's center line.*

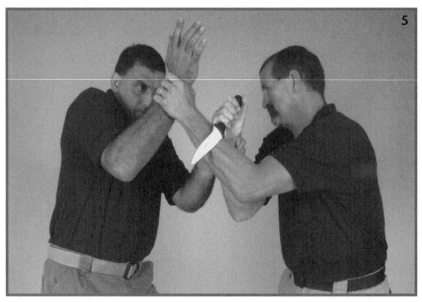

The defender utilizes the attacker's grip on his strong side hand to raise the attacker's support arm up and lodge it between himself and the attacker's blade.

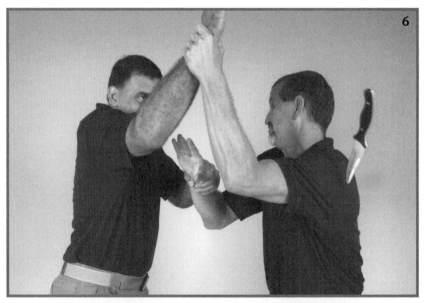

Pulling the attacker's knife hand toward himself while pushing the attacker's support hand away, the defender successfully releases the knife from the attacker's grip.

Releasing the attacker's now-empty strong side hand, the defender uses his support side hand to push the attacker's support side hand away, clearing a path for a distraction strike to the attacker's head with his strong side elbow.

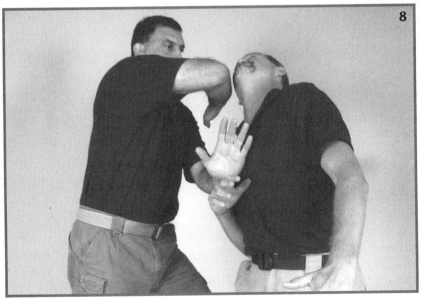

The defender completes the release technique with an elbow to the attacker's head.

Release #3:

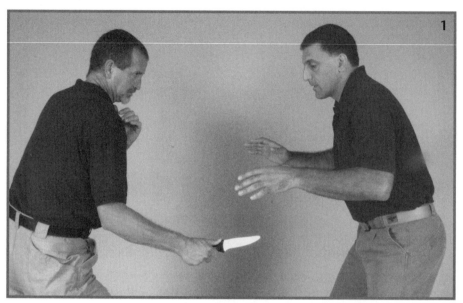

The attack comes in at contact range. There is
no choice but to defend by going hands on.

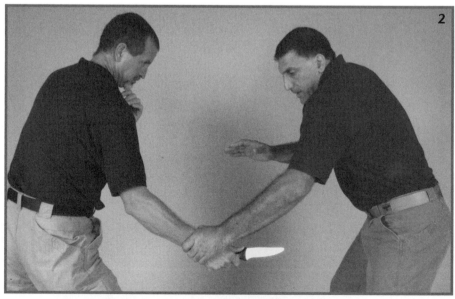

As the thrust comes in you are successfully
able to grab your attacker's weapon arm.

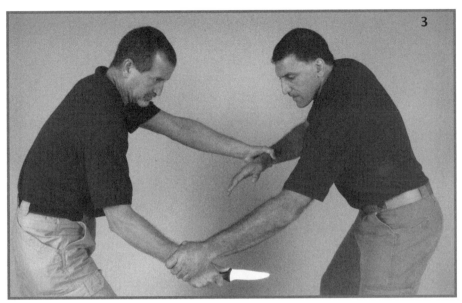

*The attacker in turn grabs your arm minimizing
your ability to defend yourself.*

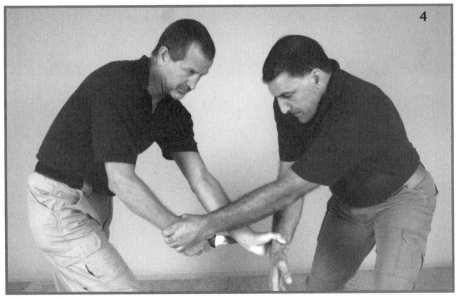

*Use your attacker's grip against him by utilizing it to pull his arm
across your center line and place his arm against the blade.*

Push his forearm against the blade as you pull his hand in the exact opposite direction thereby ejecting the blade from his grip.

Using the inertia from the disarm to break free of his grip, use your strong side arm to raise his arm up exposing his rib cage.

Proceed to rain thunderous strikes to his exposed
rib cage to complete defending yourself.

Release #4:

The attack comes in at contact range. There is
no choice but to defend by going hands on.

The defender disables the incoming thrusting
attack by grabbing the attacker's knife arm.

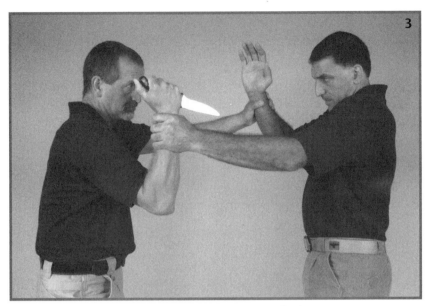

The attacker grabs the defender's arm.

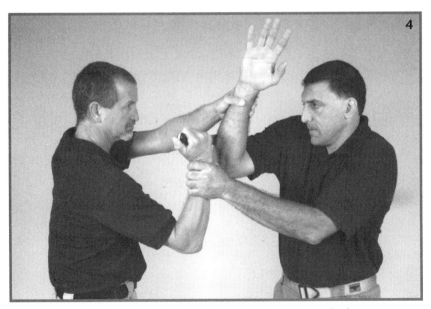

*The defender raises his strong side arm and places
the flat of the blade against the outside
of his strong side arm.*

Pulling the attacker's knife hand forward while pushing his strong side arm away, the defender successfully releases the knife from the attacker's grip.

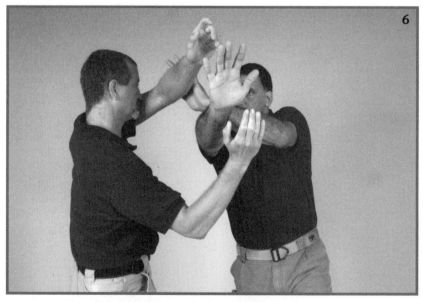

The defender successfully gets to the green zone outside the attacker's reach.

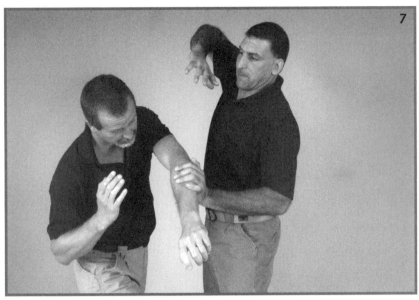

From the safety of the green zone the defender sets up an elbow strike.

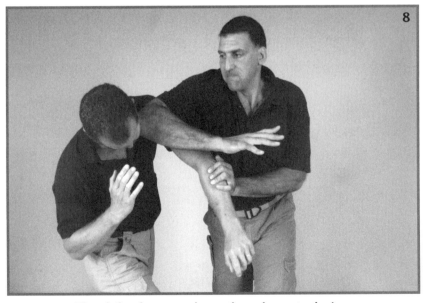

The defender completes the release technique with an elbow strike to the attacker's head.

Release #5:

At contact range, the defender faces an edged
weapon attack in the reverse grip configuration.

The defender successfully disables the incoming high line thrusting
attack by protecting his head and neck with raised forearms.

With his support side hand wedged under the flat of the blade,
the defender applies an eye strike distraction to the
attacker with his strong side hand.

Combining a hip pivot and downward scooping hand motion,
the defender successfully breaks the attacker's balance.

*Continuing the scooping motion, the defender further
breaks his attacker's balance and his grip on the weapon.*

*The weapon is released from the attacker's grip
by continuing the scooping motion.*

With the weapon successfully released from the attacker's grip, the defender delivers an elbow strike to the attacker's head.

As the attacker is bent forward by the elbow strike, the defender sets up a follow up knee strike.

The defender completes the release technique with a knee strike to the side of the attacker's head.

Release #6:

At contact range, the defender is faced with an incoming
high line thrusting attack in the reverse grip configuration.

The defender successfully disables the incoming attack
with raised forearms protecting his head and neck.

Using his support hand to retain control of the attacker's knife hand, the defender applies an eye strike distraction with his strong hand.

The defender withdraws his strong hand in preparation to release the weapon from the attacker's grip.

*The defender places the flat of the blade against
the outside of his strong side forearm.*

*The defender successfully releases the knife from
the attacker's grip, and uses the releasing motion
to apply a strike to the attacker's throat.*

The defender continues forward with his throat strike while simultaneously using his support hand to apply a wrist lock, further breaking the attacker's balance.

The defender completes the release technique with a shin kick to the attacker's groin.

Release #7:

The defender is at contact range, no time or space to get away.
He must go hands on against a low line thrusting
attack in the reverse grip configuration.

The defender disables the incoming attack by grabbing
the attacker's hand with his strong hand and
the attacker's elbow with his support hand.

The defender brings his support side
forearm above the weapon.

The defender places the flat of the blade
against his support side forearm.

The defender successfully releases the weapon from the attacker's grip by pulling up on the attacker's weapon hand while simultaneously pushing his forearm against the flat of the blade.

Maintaining his grip on the attacker's arm, the defender breaks the attacker's balance forward toward the floor, while preparing to deliver a shin kick.

*The defender completes the release technique
with a shin kick to the attacker's head.*

Release #8:

The defender finds himself at contact range with an edged
weapon attack in the standard grip configuration.

The defender disables the incoming low line
thrusting attack by angling off the line of attack
and deflecting the thrust with his support hand.

*Maintaining control with his support hand, the defender
adds an eye strike distraction to his attacker
with his strong hand.*

*Controlling the attacker's knife hand with his support hand
the defender angles away from the blade giving
him some necessary room to work.*

*The defender maintains control of the attacker's knife hand
with his support hand while he brings his strong hand
into position for the release.*

*Using the back of his forearm, the defender successfully
releases the weapon from the attacker's hand and continues
forward on line to striking the attacker's face.*

*The defender completes the release technique
with a strike to the attacker's face.*

Release #9:

The defender is at contact range, it's too late to run
from this incoming high line thrusting attack.

Keeping his strong hand raised for added protection,
the defender angles off the line of attack and disables the
incoming thrusting attack with his support hand.

*Maintaining control with the support hand, the defender
reaches over the blade and applies an eye strike
distraction with his strong hand.*

*The defender uses his strong hand to control
the attacker's knife hand.*

*The defender maintains his strong hand grip
and places the back of his support side forearm
against the flat of the blade.*

*Pulling the blade toward him while pushing his forearm
against the flat of the blade, the defender successfully
ejects the weapon from the attacker's hand.*

The defender continues forward with the motion of his support hand applying a throat strike.

Using his support hand to control the attacker's neck, the defender prepares an elbow strike.

The defender completes the release technique with an elbow strike to the attacker's head.

Release #10:

At contact range the defender faces an imminent threat from an attacker with an edged weapon in the standard configuration.

The defender disables the incoming high line slashing attack by stepping inside the attacker's range and raising his forearms to protect his head and neck.

Maintaining his support hand in a defensive position, the defender applies and eye strike distraction with his strong hand.

The defender clears the weapon to the outside, getting himself to the safety of the green zone.

The defender maintains his strong hand grip on the attacker's knife hand and applies a second eye strike distraction to the attacker with his support hand.

The defender maintains his strong hand grip on the attacker's weapon hand and places his support side forearm against the flat of the blade similar to a return to sender.

By pulling the blade toward himself and pushing his support side arm forward, the defender successfully releases the blade from the attacker's grip.

The defender continues the forward motion with his support side arm and applies a distraction to the attacker's throat.

The defender completes the release technique with an elbow strike to the attacker's head.

Release #11:

The defender is at contact range and must effectively
defend a highline backhand slashing attack.

The defender successfully disables the incoming attack
by stepping off the line of attack and raising
his forearms to protect his head and neck.

*Maintaining control with his strong hand, the defender
applies an eye strike distraction with his support hand.*

*The defender now utilizes his support hand to aid
in controlling the attacker's weapon hand.*

Pulling the blade toward himself and pushing his support hand away successfully releases the weapon from the attacker's grip.

The defender extends his support hand forward to strike and further off balance the attacker.

7

With the attacker further off balance, the defender prepares an elbow strike.

8

The defender delivers an elbow strike to the attacker's head.

9

The defender completes the release technique with a knee to the attacker's mid-section.

Release #12:

At contact range with no time or space to get away, the defender
faces his attacker in a stable fighting platform with hands high.

The defender effectively disables the incoming hooking thrust
to the low line with his support hand while simultaneously
applying an eye strike distraction with his strong hand.

*Maintaining control with his support hand,
the defender uses his strong hand to maximize
his control of the attacker's weapon hand.*

*The defender applies a wristlock to break the attacker's
balance and weaken his grip on the weapon.*

*The defender uses his support hand to retain control
of the attacker's weapon hand and places his strong
side forearm against the flat of the weapon.*

*By pulling the blade toward himself and pushing his strong hand
in the other direction against the flat of the blade, the defender
successfully releases the weapon from the attacker's grip.*

The defender retains the wrist lock position with his support hand and uses his strong hand to control the attacker's neck while he prepares to deliver a knee strike.

The defender completes the release technique with a knee strike to the attacker's head.

Release #13:

*At contact range with no choice but to engage,
the defender prepares for a backhand,
low line slashing attack.*

2

The defender simultaneously disables the attacker's incoming slashing attack with his strong hand and delivers an eye strike distraction with his support hand.

3

The defender uses his support hand to control the attacker's weapon hand and prepares his strong hand for the release.

The defender places his strong side forearm against the flat of the blade.

By levering the flat of the blade against his strong side forearm, the defender successfully releases the weapon from the attacker's grip.

Continuing his motion forward, the defender uses his strong hand to strike the attacker's face.

Maintaining the wristlock control, the defender weaves his strong arm underneath the attacker's now weaponless knife arm.

8

The defender completes the release technique with a palm strike to the attacker's face.

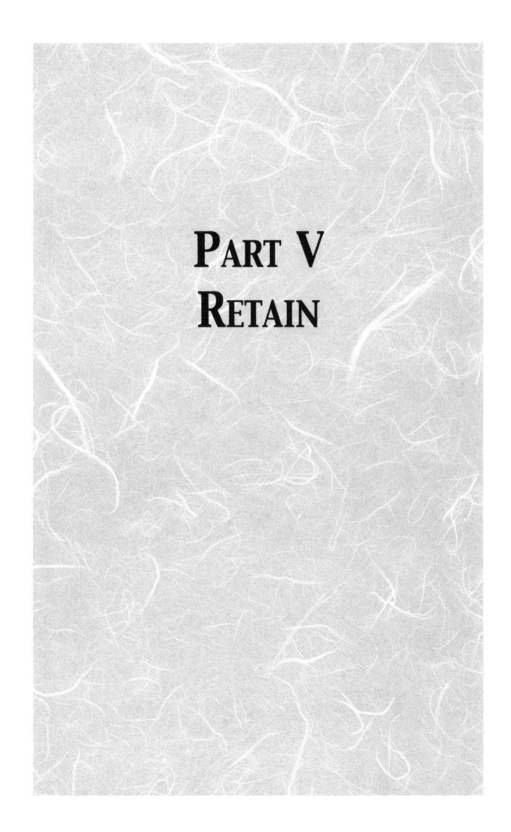

PART V
RETAIN

Now at the juncture of completion of the *Return* (beginning) and *Release* (intermediate) components of the art of disarming, we can move forward to the final component (for this manuscript—there are others) which is often referred to as *Retain*.

It does need to be mentioned again that retaining the weapon after forcibly removing it from the hand of your attack is considered an extremely high level of operational skill and is certainly not recommended—even for the most seasoned of practitioners. However, offered as a high-level component of the art of disarming, these techniques must be as comfortable as tying your shoes when your training partner strikes at you with maximum speed and force.

Retain #1:

The attack is an upward angled thrust coming in at contact range. There is no choice but to defend by going hands on.

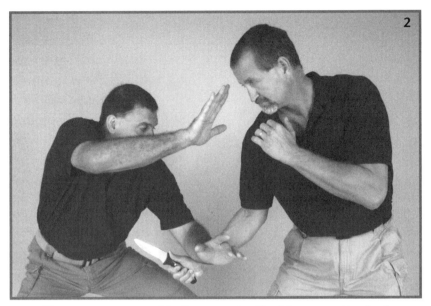

*Use your support side forearm to disable your attacker's
thrust while simultaneously distracting him with
an eye thrust with your strong side hand.*

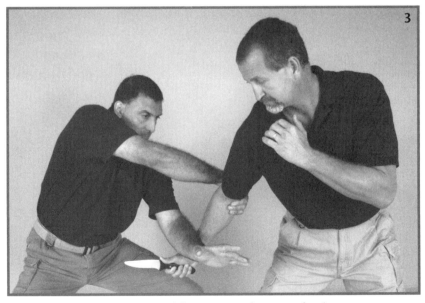

*Keep your support side arm on the attacker's weapon
side wrist and move your strong side hand to
behind his weapon side elbow.*

4 Break your attacker's balance by pulling his elbow to you while you push your hand underneath his arm.

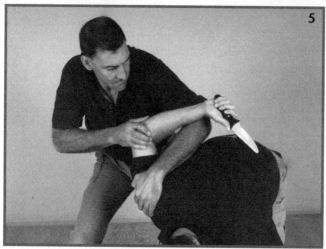

5 Complete your control position by pushing your support hand through enough to grab his shoulder and lodge the weapon hand behind his lower back.

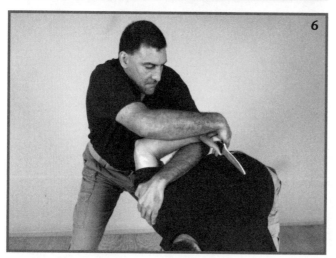

6 Use your strong side hand to bring your attacker's weapon side palm to the inside of his forearm to weaken his grip.

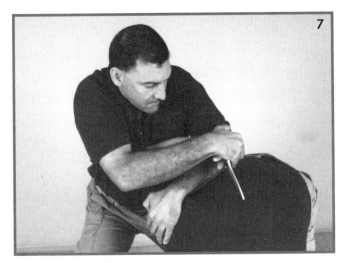

7

Keep your opponent off balance while you continue weakening his grip on the weapon.

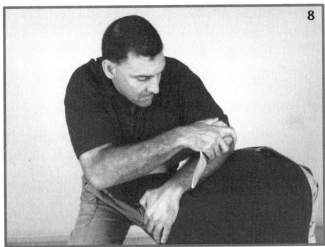

8

Using your pinky finger as a grip reference at the point where the handle meets the blade, begin to peel the weapon from your attacker's hand.

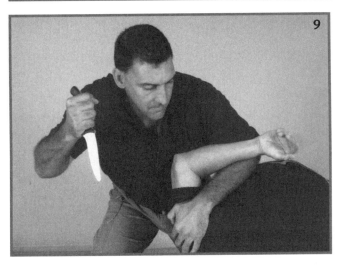

9

Complete the removal of the weapon from your attacker's hand and retain the weapon in your strong side hand.

Retain #2:

At contact range with no time or space to escape, the defender prepares himself for the fight in a stable fighting platform.

The attacker strikes with a forehand high line thrusting attack in the reverse grip configuration which the defender disables by raising his arms to protect his head and neck, simultaneously wedging his support arm between the flat of the blade and the attacker's wrist.

The defender utilizes this wedged position to break the attacker's balance and weaken his grip while delivering an eye strike distraction with his strong hand.

The defender adds his strong hand to the task of gripping to gain maximum control of the weapon, and places his wrist near the handle of the blade in preparation for the retain technique.

*Close up shot shows proper placement of the weapon
in relation to the defender's support hand.*

*Maintaining his strong hand grip, the defender
releases his support hand so he can grip the weapon
once it is released from the attacker's hand.*

Continuing through the scooping motion, the defender successfully releases the weapon from the attacker's grip, retains it in his support hand and maintains his off balancing grip on the attacker's now weaponless hand.

The defender completes the retain technique and has the option to utilize the attacker's blade against him.

Retain #3:

At contact range, the defender assumes a stable
fighting platform to deal with an edged weapon
attack in the reverse grip configuration.

The defender successfully disables the incoming high line thrusting attack by raising his forearms to protect his head and neck.

The defender wedges his support hand between the flat of the blade and the attacker's wrist while delivering an eye strike distraction with his strong hand.

Maintaining contact control with his strong hand, the defender places his support hand in position to receive the released weapon.

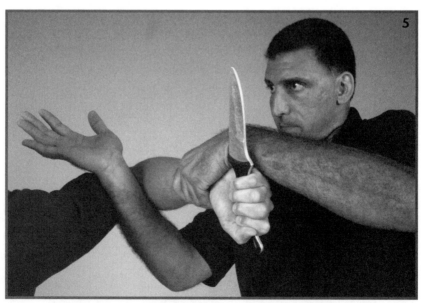

Close up shot from the reverse angle shows the proper placement of the defender's hands in relation to the attacker's weapon and weapon arm.

The defender retains the attacker's weapon and pushes the attacker off with his strong hand getting further into the green zone outside the attacker's arms.

Getting to the attacker's back, the defender has the option to complete the retain technique by using the attacker's weapon against him.

Retain #4:

Faced with an incoming edged weapon attack in the reverse grip configuration at contact range, the defender assumes a stable fighting platform and instantly changes from victim to victor.

The defender successfully defends the highline thrusting attack by raising his forearms to protect his head and neck.

*The defender wedges his support arm between the flat
of the blade and the attacker's wrist while simultaneously
applying an eye strike distraction with his strong hand.*

*The defender utilizes the attacker's grip on the weapon to keep him
off balance. He also places his strong hand in position to retain
the weapon once it is released from the attacker's grip.*

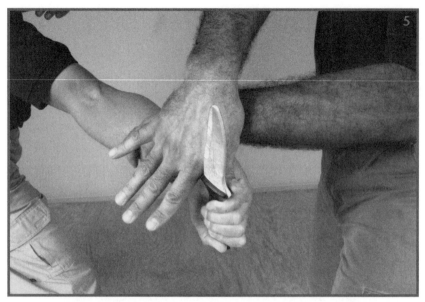

Close up shot of proper hand placement in relation to the attacker's weapon in order to retain the weapon once it is released from the attacker's grip.

The defender uses his strong hand to retain the weapon once it is released from the attacker's grip.

*It is sometimes necessary to apply a defensive strike
with the attacker's weapon.*

*The defender completes the retain technique and is prepared
for another defensive strike with the weapon should it be
necessary to end the threat that the attacker presents.*

Retain #5:

The defender assumes
a stable fighting platform
to defend a contact range
edged weapon attack
in the reverse grip
configuration.

The defender successfully
disables the incoming
backhand high line
thrusting attack by
raising his forearms
to protect his head
and neck.

Using his support hand to control the attacker's knife hand, the defender simultaneously uses his strong hand to apply an eye strike distraction.

The defender uses both hands to maximize control of the attacker's weapon hand.

The defender maintains his support hand grip on the attacker's weapon hand and places his strong hand in position to retain the weapon once it is released from the attacker's grip.

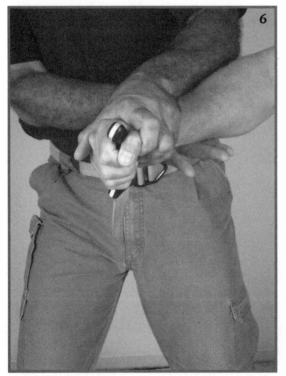

Close up shot shows the proper position of the defender's hands to maximize control of the attacker's knife hand and prepare to retain the weapon once it is released.

The defender releases the weapon from the attacker's grip and retains the weapon in his strong hand.

The defender completes the retain technique by off balancing the attacker with his support hand wrist lock while using the weapon to end the threat posed by the attacker.

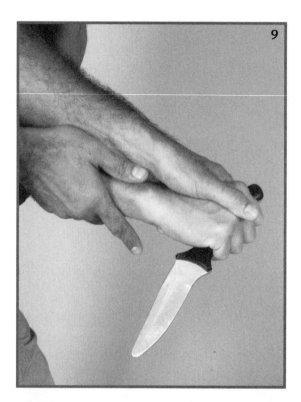

This sequence of shots shows the proper placement of the hands in order to retain the weapon once it is released from the attacker's grip.

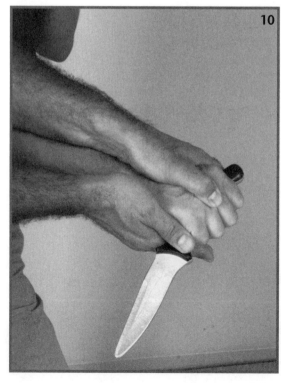

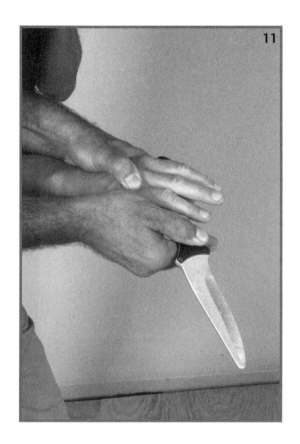

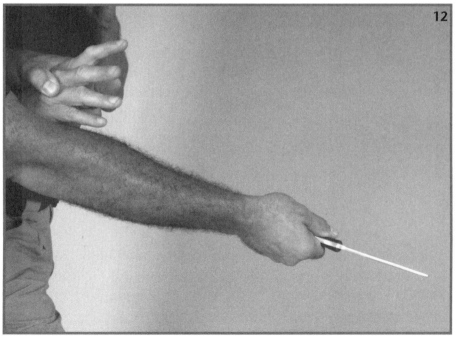

Retain #6

Faced with an edged weapon attack at contact range, the defender assumes a stable fighting platform.

The defender disables the incoming thrusting attack by stepping off the line of attack while deflecting the attacker's weapon arm with his support hand.

Maintaining control of the attacker's weapon arm with his support hand, the defender applies an eye strike distraction with his strong hand.

The defender gains a solid grip on the attacker's knife hand with his support hand.

5

The defender prepares his strong hand to retain the weapon once it is extracted from the attacker's grip.

6

By pulling up with his support hand and pushing down with his strong hand, the defender successfully releases the knife from the attacker's grip and retains it in his strong hand.

7

The defender utilizes the weapon to influence a bend in the attacker's strong side arm.

8

The defender weaves his support side arm under the attacker's strong side arm to gain underhook control and is prepared to deliver follow up strikes with the weapon if necessary.

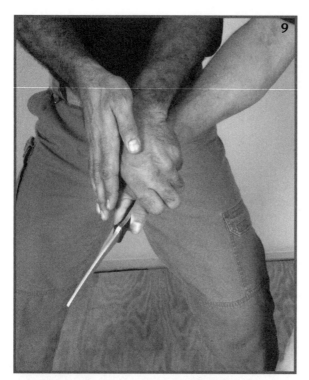

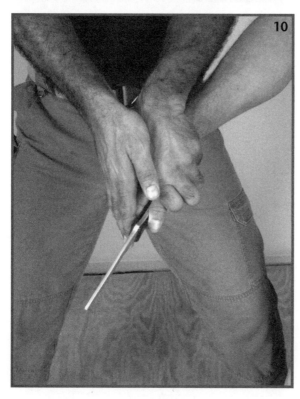

This sequence shows the proper placement of the defender's hands on the attacker's knife hand in order to successfully extract the weapon from the attacker's grip and retain it in his strong hand.

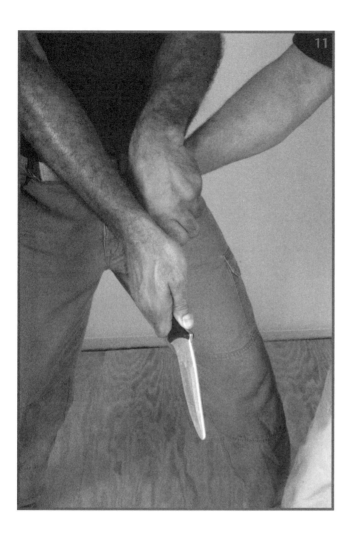

Retain #7:

*The defender assumes a stable fighting platform
when faced with an imminent high line thrusting
attack in the standard grip configuration.*

The defender successfully disables the incoming thrusting attack by stepping off the line of attack while using his support hand to deflect the attacker's weapon arm.

The defender applies an eye strike distraction with his strong hand.

*The defender maximizes his control with his strong hand
grip on the attacker's knife hand and his support hand
on the attacker's weapon arm elbow.*

*The defender places both hands on the attacker's knife hand,
overpowers the attacker's grip and points the blade
at the attacker, away from himself.*

The defender begins a return to sender on the attacker.

*The defender successfully retains the weapon in his
support hand and completes the retain technique
by applying a defensive strike to his attacker.*

Retain #8:

Faced with an edged weapon attack at contact range, with no time
or space to run, the defender assumes a stable fighting platform.

The defender disables the incoming attack by stepping inside the
attacker's power and raising his arms to protect his head and neck.

*The defender applies an eye strike distraction
with his strong hand.*

*The defender clears his body to the green zone
outside the attacker's weapon arm.*

*Maintaining a solid grip on the attacker's knife hand
with his strong hand, the defender applies a second
eye strike distraction with his support hand.*

*The defender uses both hands on the attacker's weapon hand
to maximize his control of the attacker's weapon hand and
places his support hand in position to retain the weapon.*

*The defender extracts and retains the weapon from the attacker
and delivers a defensive strike with the weapon.*

*The defender completes the retain technique with a second
defensive strike with the attacker's weapon.*

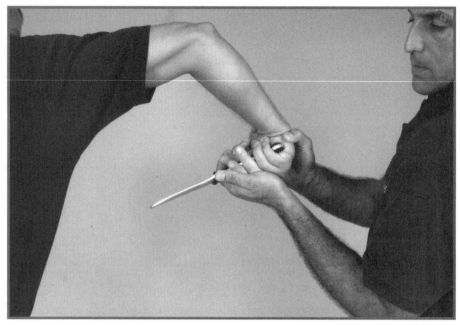

*This sequence shows the proper placement of the
hands for maximum control and efficiency
of utilizing this retain technique.*

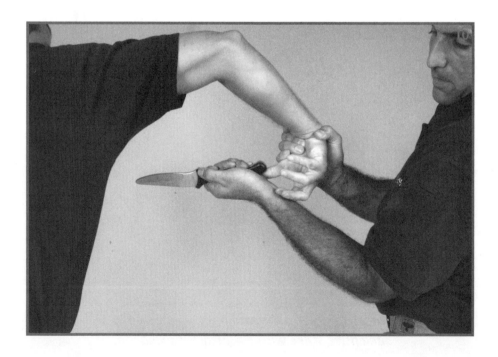

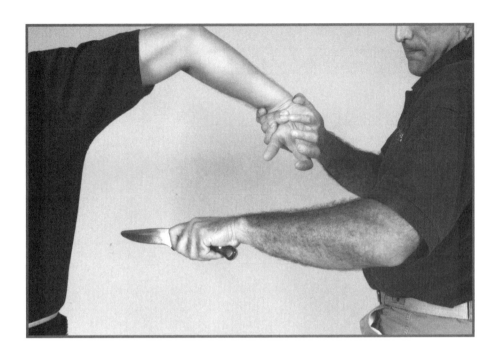

Retain #9:

At contact range the defender is faced with an incoming high line backhand edged weapon attack.

*The defender successfully disables the incoming attack
by raising his forearms to defend his head and neck.*

*The defender controls the attacker's knife hand with his strong hand
while delivering an eye strike distraction with his support hand.*

With his strong hand already in position, the defender places his support side forearm against the attacker's knife arm in preparation of retaining the weapon.

Using his support side forearm to push the attacker's knife arm away, the defender successfully extracts and retains the attacker's weapon.

*While using his support side arm to off balance the attacker,
the defender prepares a defensive strike with the retained weapon.*

*The defender completes the retain technique
with a defensive strike.*

This sequence shows the proper placement of the hands for executing this retain technique.

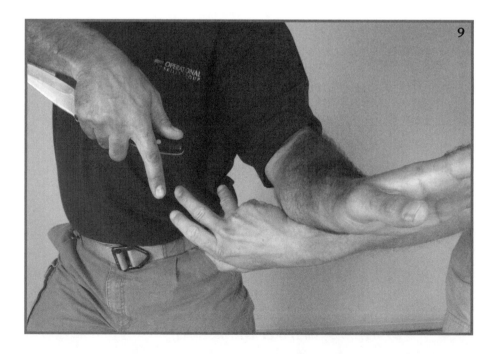

Retain #10:

The defender assumes a stable fighting platform to deal with the incoming contact range edged weapon attack.

The defender disables the incoming low line hooking thrust attack with his support hand while simultaneously applying an eye strike distraction with his strong hand.

The defender uses both hands to maximize
his control of the attacker's knife hand.

The defender applies a wrist lock to break the
attacker's balance and grip on the weapon.

*The defender places his strong hand in position
to retain the weapon once extracted.*

*The defender completes the retain technique with
a defensive strike with the attacker's weapon.*

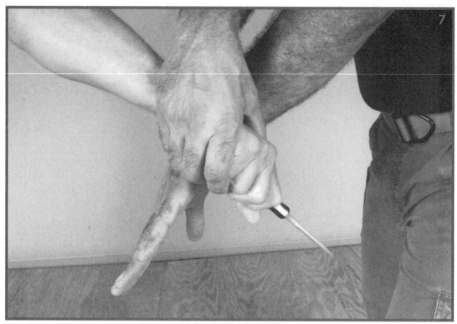

This sequence shows the proper placement of the hands to maximize control and efficiency in completing this retain technique.

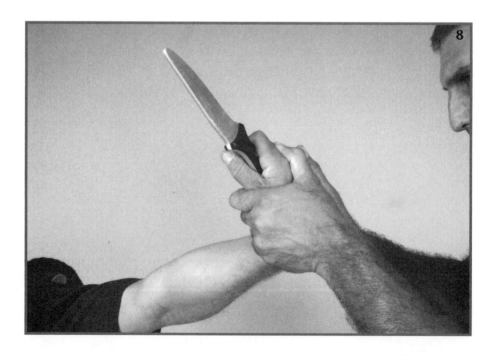

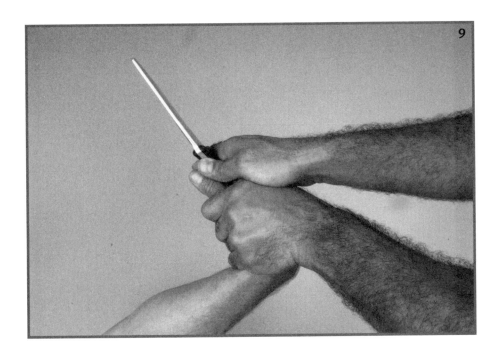

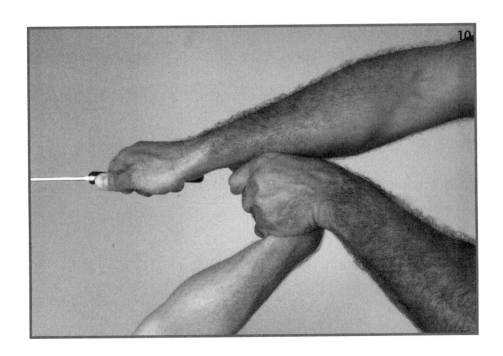

Retain #11:

The defender is faced with an edged weapon attack at contact range, with no time or space to get away he assumes a stable fighting platform.

The defender successfully disables the incoming low line back hand slashing attack with his strong hand while simultaneously applying an eye strike distraction with his support hand.

The defender controls the attacker's knife hand grip with his support hand.

The defender places his strong hand in position to extract and retain the weapon.

5 The defender breaks the attacker's balance while successfully extracting and retaining the weapon.

6 The defender completes the retain technique with a defensive strike to the attacker's body.

PART VI
SCENARIOS

Upon the completion of our study of the isolated components of the art of disarming, it is incumbent upon the serious student to practice for many hours and days on end to build familiarization and then eventually proficiency.

The masters tell us that it takes about 3,000 repetitions of a single technique to "attain beginning level." It takes another 3,000 to 4,000 repetitions to gain proficiency and then yet another 3,000 to 4,000 repetitions to gain the experience and skill necessary to be able to use it in a real-life scenario. If you do the math, that's about 10,000 reps.

In my personal experience it took almost 25 years, at least ten hours per week hammering through technique after technique and repeating them over and over and over and over again both at a slow and controlled rate and then at higher speeds. To this very day—several decades later there are very few of these that I would in fact trust my life to—only because (unlike the masters) I have not yet fully internalized each movement as natural as breathing. Still working on it though!

The end goal of all this training is to take the isolated component techniques (Return, Release and Retain) and be able to internalize them enough to be able to apply them in real world scenarios.

The reader is reminded that this is an art and like any art (music, dance, painting, acting, etc) the art of disarming cannot be mastered in one sitting. It takes time to cultivate understanding and familiarization with the concepts and techniques. Only with much time and endless practice can true familiarization and understanding be increased to a level of proficiency applicable to real-world application.

The following block of training is designed from most commonly reported knife attacks and is intended as a proficiency training tool. The following scenarios are presented in such a manner as to add a layer of practical application (how the isolated techniques might be applied in the real world) to take our training level to the next step of proficiency.

Scenario #1

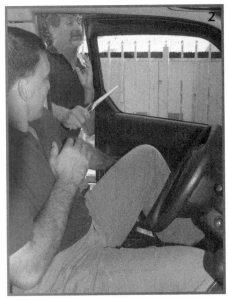

The defender is surprised in
a confined area of operations.
He can't get away, he must
defend himself immediately.

Utilizing the car door,
the defender successfully limits
the attacker's ability to reach
him with the edged weapon.

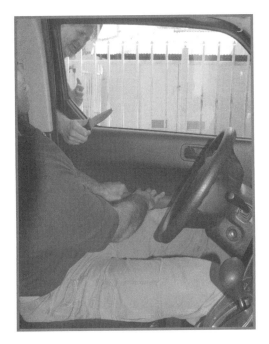

The defender uses the car
door to distract the attacker
by slamming it on his arm.

Scenario #2:

The defender is in a confined area of operations again, but this time the door is closed and the window is open.

As the attacker tries to reach in through the window, the defender begins to roll it up minimizing the attacker's reach.

The defender successfully disables the incoming attack by rolling the window up on the attacker's arm.

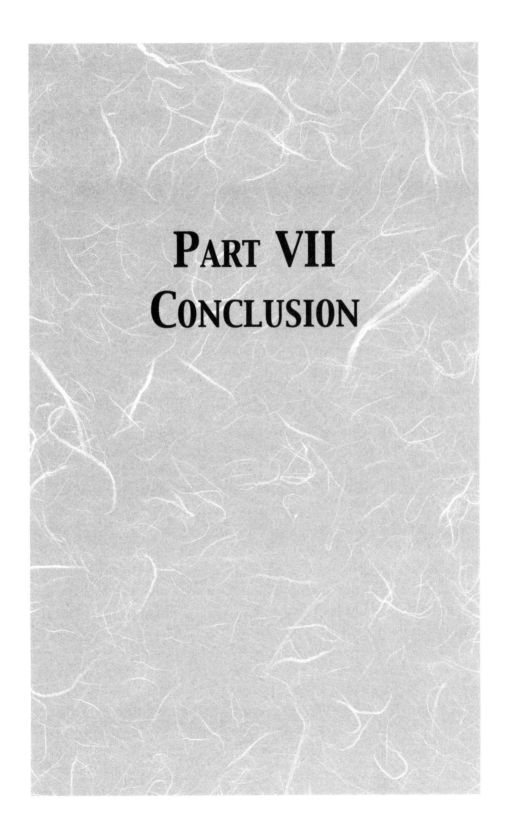

PART VII
CONCLUSION

When faced with an edged weapon attack, it is essential to keep it all in perspective.

Real life is not the movies. Remember, everything in this book is dependent upon there being *no safe exit*. The material presented here is only applicable when *you have no remaining options* but to stay and fight. You don't have a gun, you have nowhere to move—no space and no time and you don't have any backup whatsoever (family, friends, the cavalry is NOT about to come riding up over the hill). Further, you are unable to Exit or Equalize—you have no other options but to either bleed out and die or apply a disarming technique.

Human bodies can be cut or punctured very easily. How many times have you cut yourself shaving, got a paper cut or cut your fingers open with some sharp object? Now imagine a ruthless attacker wielding an edged weapon intent on purposefully cutting you open! The real answer is to get away—exit. Don't put your body in the path of an incoming edged weapon in the first place.

If there's any possibility whatsoever that you can get away, doing so in the most expedient manner possible is your best option. If you cannot exit (the safest defense option) then equalize—get something in your hands to defend yourself with as soon as possible. Common techniques are to remove one of your shoes, take off your belt or a jacket or even your shirt, wrap it or hold it in your hand and use it to deflect the incoming weapon. Even if only for a split second, it can buy you the time and space that you need to exit as quickly as possible. It is only when you have *no other choice* but to engage your threat with your bare hands should any attempt be made (at your own risk) utilizing any of the techniques described in this book be viable.

Remember what the masters have passed down to us—proficiency is learned over time with proper practice, and repetition is the mother of all skills. Without the necessary repetitions there is little or no skill. Consequently, with little or no skill there is little or no confidence in the application of these techniques even in isolated training, let alone in a practical application scenario! With that in mind, let's summarize the key components of our training.

Exit or Equalize—this is the VERY best reaction and is considered the optimal response to a real world assault scenario. The better of these is Exit as this places distance between you and your attacker which buys you time to get out. This is the safest option as it reduces personal injury to just about zero. Not as optimal (but certainly better than trying to apply a fancy disarming technique!) is to equalize the playing field. Get something in your hand or hands as quickly as possible. Any object striking the blade will be better than catching the blade with your bare hands. Although you may increase your Scale of Injury utilizing this option, as it is not as safe as Exit, at least you will hopefully sustain low-level injuries (if any) and enable you to go back to Plan "A"—get out of there (Exit) as quickly as possible!

Barring the Exit or Equalize option remember the key combative concept of: Distract, Disable and Disarm. If you can disable the incoming attack and get away, that is the best solution (following Exit and Equalize). If you are close enough to distract the attacker with a defensive strike of some kind and then get away, that is also a viable option. Strike or Control—keep in mind your training on *striking* or *controlling* the weapon arm. Again, these are the safest options which can effectively reduce the Scale of Injury.

Last but not least is the actual disarming technique itself. Considered by the masters as a last ditch effort (either *accidental or incidental),* if the scenario or the attacker's persistence give you no other choice but attempt a disarm technique rather than take it across the throat or in the belly (disarm or die), then keep in mind our three isolated training component groups: Return (beginning skill level), Release (intermediate skill level), and Retain (advanced training—not recommended without a very high level of proficiency).

ART VERSUS APPLICATION

The art of disarming is just that—an art. As mentioned above, like any art it takes years, decades, and by higher standards (the masters) literally a lifetime to truly master. There's no way a reader of this book with zero prior training in the bladed arts will be able to read this material once and then with zero practice pick up a couple of tricks and go out and utilize them tonight at the local bar.

The material contained herein is designed for those interested from an historical perspective in the ancient bladed arts (with regards to the ancient art of disarming) as well as the serious student of the knife who is willing and able to take the time to train, practice and execute the literally thousands and thousands of repetitions that it takes to gain a practical level of proficiency with these techniques.

To further support this proficiency issue, in a recent course I delivered to a certain group of operators, a student posed the question: "Well, yeah these techniques all look good on paper, on the DVD and in slow motion, but they're carefully choreographed and with control can be practiced, but what about an attacker trying to rip your head off in real life?" This is my exact point. In fact I couldn't have stated my "Art versus Application" concept any better if I tried. The answer is familiarization, repetitions which increase skill level, and finally sustainment of those skills. Similar to an individual who's never held a firearm in his hand, how can that person be expected to simply read a book and without any training or practice, master the skills of gun-handing and marksmanship in practical application?

Let's revisit our previous example of that professional basketball player. Alone and with no pressure and no other players he can stand on that line and sink baskets all day. But now add aggressive opponents and the pressure of a full-court press, now add even more pressure that it's a playoff game for all the marbles. Will that same player be able to hit those same baskets under extreme duress *every single time?* Of course not. The same exact thing applies to these techniques. If a student practices to the point of proficiency he may be able to successfully pull off the technique for real (when it really counts) to some percentage—it will never be exact, it will never look pretty, it will never be 100 per cent and it will never be easy under pressure. However, what's the alternative? If you have no training whatsoever (zero technique or repetitions), and you cannot exit or equalize, distract or disarm and you have no other remaining options other than to stand there and get your throat slit open and die, what choice do you have?

The answer is to always be ready. You never know when or how or where or why or even if it will ever happen. It is my intention by placing this material in written manuscript form and presenting it in a layered instructional format, that it will at least provide yet another tool in your personal defense tool kit—an ace in your back pocket if you may ever need it for real.

Stay safe and stay trained,
Steve Tarani
August 2007

ABOUT THE AUTHOR

Subject matter expert (SME) advisor to US FBI, US DEA, US TSA and other agencies as well as an active federal use-of-force training contractor utilized by US DOJ, US DHS, US DOD, etc. Steve Tarani is a full-time training provider of operational skills to high-profile agencies. His programs of instruction have been accepted as standard curriculum for a number of US federal and state-accredited programs.

Author Steve Tarani lecturing on operational readiness.

Possessing unique knowledge and information valuable to the enabling of skills in the area of edged weapon personal defense, Tarani is considered a leading subject matter authority in the professional training community.

A devoted disciple of the masters of the bladed arts for more than a quarter of a century, Mr. Tarani is uniquely certified in four (4) specific documented systems: Bahala Na (Graduate Instructor), Inosanto Academy of Martial Arts (Instructor), LAMECO Eskrima (Instructor) and Mande Muda (Instructor). His decades of devotion as a disciple of his Filipino, Malaysian and Indonesian masters set him apart from other instructors. In addition to his unbroken years of study with his masters who migrated to the US, Tarani has also trained directly under the lineage of his masters on-site in Japan, the Philippines, and Indonesia.

Notes _____